THE SEVENTH CIRCLE

Surviving seven years in Afghanistan's most notorious prison

ROB LANGDON

ALLEN&UNWIN

First published in Great Britain in 2017 by Allen & Unwin
First published in Australia in 2017 by Allen & Unwin
Copyright © Rob Langdon, 2017

Allen & Unwin
c/o Atlantic Books
Ormond House
26–27 Boswell Street
London WC1N 3JZ

Phone: 020 7269 1610
Fax: 020 7430 0916
Email: UK@allenandunwin.com
Web: www.allenandunwin.com/uk

A CIP catalogue record of this book is available from
the British Library.

Paperback ISBN 978 1 76029 690 2
E-book ISBN 978 1 92557 567 5

Set in 11.5/15 t Sabon by Midland Typesetters, Australia
Printed in Great Britain by CPI Group (UK) Ltd Croydon CR0 4YY

10 9 8 7 6 5 4 3 2 1

Contents

Author's note

Where friends or colleagues remain operational, I've used their initials in order to protect their identities. Other names have been changed to protect the guilty. You know who you are.

PART ONE

PART ONE

Dead Men

2009–2010

1

The arrest

Here's how close I was to getting away.

Minutes. Maybe five, maybe three, stood between me and getting on the plane. I had got to Kabul International Airport and walked through check-in without luggage or any possessions other than the clothes on my back and the packages of American dollars in my pockets. I was cleared through customs and several security gates in the clean, newly built terminal. My flight on Afghanistan's national carrier, Safi Airways, to Dubai was on time, and I made it through the departure lounge where I showed my boarding pass and waited with the other passengers for the minibus to take us to the plane sitting on the tarmac. All that was left was a quick shuttle to the steps of the jet and I was home free.

Just a few hundred seconds. As long as a cupful of water takes to boil. How many times, over the next seven years, could I shut my eyes and count out those seconds? How many prison kettles of water would that add up to? In what kind of a blink could they pass, compared with the black hole that would chew the next seven years out of my life? If I thought about that too much, I could drive myself mad.

I kept my head down, not looking at the other passengers, just willing the minibus to come and take us to the plane. After the chaos of the previous twenty-four hours, I was more strung-out with fatigue than panicky or scared. I was composed but tired, thinking only one thought: *Let's go.* I wore my Blundstones and a checked shirt and jeans that I'd picked up earlier in the day from my mate Frank, whose place I'd dropped into during the height of the mayhem. Frank, a Canadian freelance security contractor I'd worked with for years in Afghanistan and Iraq, and I had talked about which airport I should go to. One option was the airfield at Bagram, the military base where I could get onto an American military aircraft. Bagram had its advantages, being under American control, and as a security contractor working for an American company, I had come and gone freely from Bagram over the previous twelve months with identification that gave me the equivalent rank to a captain. Frank made a plan to get me there. But I was wary of Bagram. The drive was too far for comfort, and the security would be intense. Any of numerous checkpoints could pull me up. My preference was for Kabul International, the civilian airport. I had bought the Safi Airways ticket for Dubai the previous day, before all hell broke loose. A day ago, I had expected to be flying out of Afghanistan for the last time on my way to starting a new adventure in Africa. It might as well have been a lifetime ago. In twenty-four hours, everything had changed.

Bagram or Kabul International? US military or Afghan civilian? In the end, I did what I always did when faced with a fifty-fifty decision. I pulled my trusty Australian fifty-cent coin out of my pocket and tossed it.

Heads. Kabul International.

Frank wished me luck as I left his place in a taxi. I got to the airport without incident. Like a lot of major infrastructure in the city, Kabul International was fitted out with the latest computerised equipment, but the locals didn't know how to use or maintain half of it. It looked nice, but everywhere you looked were half-finished offices, rubbish blowing around, and computers still in their boxes. The grand opening for international civilian flights, just a few weeks earlier, was the first stop in the airport's decline to wrack and ruin.

The security arrangements were tight, though. A British company called Global Risk Management, which employed several people I knew in the tight-knit world of private security contractors, had been teaching the Afghans how to do airport security, and they were efficient. I was inspected, scanned and searched at two gates after passport control. I went down a set of stairs to the departure lounge, and as I was waiting for the call to board, my phone rang. The screen said it was Anton, one of the managers at work.

'It's all good,' Anton said. 'Just wait there, you'll be fine.'

I trusted Anton, in as much as I could trust anyone who'd done the things I'd seen him involved with. Actually, I didn't really know how much I could trust him. I was working that out as I went along.

Soon enough I had an answer. Another call came in. It was Elena, who worked as an administrator at Four Horsemen, the American company I had worked for in the year since I'd been in Afghanistan. Elena was the wife of Petar, the operations manager and leader of a group of Macedonians who held senior positions in Four Horsemen's

Kabul office. Elena was really good at her job and we'd had a cordial professional relationship during my year in Afghanistan. I treat people as I find them, but the Macedonians didn't like other men talking to their women, and my friendliness with Elena had never gone down very well with her husband and his mates.

'Rob, I have to warn you,' Elena said.

My heart rate went up a little. 'What's going on?'

'My husband has given the NDS passport photos of you, details about you, everything they need to identify you. They're coming for you now. You need to get out of the airport.'

Fuck. Had I been sold out? The NDS, or National Directorate of Security, Afghanistan's secret police, had close connections to Commander Haussedin, the local war lord who I believed was the main source of all of my, and our company's, problems. If Petar had sold me out to Haussedin, the next few minutes could be the difference literally between life and death. I considered my options. I couldn't go back out of the airport the way I'd come in: on the streets, I would never escape. I couldn't get to Bagram now that the alert was out. And my Safi Airways flight was only minutes from boarding. My way out of here was in that plane.

Over the next seven years, I thought about Elena's call. As I gathered more information, I eventually came to reconsider what had happened. Maybe I wasn't really seconds from getting away. Maybe it was all a set-up. Maybe that minibus would have just waited on the tarmac for however long it took for the cops to come and grab me. Maybe, as I wished for those few seconds to tick over, my fate had already been sealed by forces beyond my knowledge or control. In a strange way, that consoled me. Better to be angry at betrayal than wringing your hands over bad luck and a couple of minutes.

In the events that followed Elena's call, I had one—if only one—stroke of fortune. The eight men who came into the departure lounge to grab me, led by an officer waving around a copy of my passport photo page, my company ID and some other proof-of-life documents, were wearing uniforms. They were Afghan police, not NDS, who would have been in plain clothes. If the NDS had arrested me I would probably have been taken to a 'black' or secret prison, tortured and murdered. I'm reasonably sure that that's what would have happened if I had tried to get into Bagram.

The uniformed cops didn't tell me I was under arrest. They didn't tell me anything. Without a single word, they grabbed me by the arms and marched me back through the departure lounge. I played dumb. As we walked, I got my hand into my pocket and found the redial button on my phone. The last person I'd called was Frank, and I definitely trusted him. With my phone on and the redial button pressed, I hoped that Frank could hear what the police were telling me as they walked me through the airport. Frank would put two and two together and know I'd been caught. The most important thing was to remain visible.

As we walked, I began asking loud questions, spelling everything out so that Frank could overhear exactly what was going on.

'What are you doing?'

'Where are you taking me?'

'To police headquarters or the commander's office here?'

'Why are there eight of you who need to do that?'

When we came towards the airport security office, I had one last hope: the 'Green Line Handshake', as it was called. On the frequent previous occasions when I'd had to go through Kabul International Airport, a security officer

I knew, Captain Hamid, would help me and other security contractors avoid certain levels of scrutiny. Four Horsemen would send us to Dubai with as much as two or three hundred thousand American dollars in cash that it wanted us to hand over to Tim Akuchi, the company's Kenyan-born financial controller. For the company, it was worth spending a few grand in bribes and airfares to get hundreds of thousands out from under the tax man's nose. So we contractors would be given a return flight to Dubai, five grand to piss away while we were there, and a couple of grand for Captain Hamid and his Green Line Handshake.

I had US$12,000 on my body: $10,000 I had collected that day, in the rush to leave, from my own bank account, which I'd stashed in my pocket and in my ID holder, plus another $2000 in cash that I always carried in my wallet for emergencies. This might be my last chance. I thought my luck might be turning when Captain Hamid appeared among the uniformed men gathering outside the airport security office. My last resort was to get a private moment with him. There might be some way he could take some money and escort me back to the plane. I tried to catch his eye.

When we entered the office, that hope fell away. Sitting by the desk was Commander Haussedin. I thought, *I know where this is coming from now*. Of course. Captain Hamid was one of Haussedin's men, a fellow Panjshiri tribesman. From the Panjshir Valley north of Kabul, this small but influential tribe were key players in Afghan politics, and whichever power was in charge, be it the Americans, the Russians, the Afghan Taliban, the mujahideen or the mob of crooks installed after the American invasion, the Panjshiris always ended up on the right side of the deal. Everything dodgy, dirty and corrupt that our company did was ultimately connected to Haussedin and his Panjshiri cronies. It's a mark of my desperation that I ever entertained the thought that Captain Hamid might have been able to help me.

Haussedin—who had turned into my nemesis and enemy over the previous twelve months—was not looking particularly happy as he sat in the airport security office and watched the uniformed police go about their business. They searched me in front of the war lord and took my wallet, my passport and other ID, and the $US12,000. They pilfered my sunglasses, pretty much helping themselves to everything but my clothes. I never saw any of it again.

Haussedin became furious when they found my phone, which was still on the line to Frank. They switched it off and trousered it. Haussedin began barking at the cops. Although I couldn't understand what he was saying—throughout, they spoke only in Dari Persian—I gathered that he was unhappy that I had been taken by uniformed police rather than the NDS, and that somebody on the outside had been informed of my arrest.

Frank would, that day, call Four Horsemen to tell them where I was and what had happened to me. They said they already knew and told him to butt out of it. He had his hands full when the NDS turned up at his doorstep later, and he was forced to bullshit his way out of any suspected role in my attempted escape.

I was held in the airport security office for a couple of hours. Without an interpreter, I didn't know what was going on. I knew what they had arrested me for, but had no idea what was going to happen next. As they talked among themselves, I acted meek and mild and dumb. Now and then I asked, in English, what was going on and if I could make a phone call, but that went nowhere.

With Commander Haussedin was a man the police described, in broken English, as a 'legal representative' from Four Horsemen. But he wasn't a lawyer. My guess is he'd watched an episode of *LA Law*. He sat there obediently and did nothing other than watch.

Eventually he had some action to look at. Two plain-clothed police, who I understood to be NDS, came in. I thought, *Here we go.* I was handcuffed, thrown against the wall, searched again and photographed. The head of airport security hit me in the head, slapping me with an open hand, careful not to leave any visible damage. He was going off his brain, screaming at me, but what he was saying was surreal.

'You're a tourist!'

Whack.

'You fucking tourist!'

Whack.

'You're a tourist!'

This was so bizarre, and so stressful, and I'd been awake for I don't know how long, all I could do was start laughing. *A tourist? That was what I'd done?* I wasn't too keen on tourists myself—pretenders, idiots who swanned into Afghanistan pretending to be hard men, wannabes, fake journalists, opportunists, drug-addled aid workers, the joint was crawling with tourists. And now I was accused of being one of them. I thought, *Yeah, sure, man, I'm a tourist, just drop me at the nearest youth hostel.*

By the time I came to understand what he was really calling me—'You're a terrorist!'—every policeman in the room had taken offence at my laughter and begun hooking in. One came up and hit me in the ribs with the butt end of his rifle, which he then used to crack the side of my jaw. I felt a tooth break off. I went down onto the floor, grabbing my head. They stopped for a moment and had a discussion. I think they agreed not to hit me in the face anymore, because from then it was open season on kicking me in the ribs, arms and legs. I tucked my head in while they all took turns. Credit to them, they stayed away from my face.

Once they were done, they frogmarched me out of the office into the public area of the airport. As we went down a flight of stairs, there were a couple of Americans coming up the other way, staring at me, *What the fuck?* written on their faces.

'Yeah,' I mumbled to them as I went past. 'Bad day out for everybody, I think . . .'

The next hours blurred by. They threw me in a police van and took me to the headquarters of the counter-terrorism police in the centre of Kabul, where I was put into a cell. It was a shithole, filthy and damp and reeking of excrement, the worst you can imagine of a Middle Eastern jail cell. After a few hours, someone brought in a small bowl of rice. No water—I still hadn't drunk a drop since I was at Frank's place several hours earlier and was getting seriously dehydrated. I sat on the floor and bundled myself into a ball, my arms wrapped around my knees. I was so buggered I drifted into a half-sleep, but someone must have been on duty to make sure I didn't get comfortable, because whenever I began to drop off some men would come in and give me another touch-up, handcuffing me to a wall so my arms were above my head and then slapping and kicking me.

They kept me there for a night. The next day they moved me somewhere else in the same building and left me alone for a day or so. On the third day they grabbed me roughly and threw me into another van, which took me to a holding cell packed full of what looked like criminal suspects dragged out of holes. Rail-thin and smelling like they hadn't washed in years, these Afghans were sharing a bowl of rice like animals. They barely even noticed me. I went to a corner and tried to be invisible again. That cell was a concrete box with some thick glass tiles in a line above head height. Over the steel door was a security screen, shaped as a concertina, like a lift door, that the guards could look through. For a toilet there was only a bucket already full of shit that had overflowed onto the floor.

No doubt about it, I was fucked. The fact that I'd been given no proper lawyer, no chance to make a phone call, no contact with my employer let alone the Australian embassy or anyone who could speak English, all added up to the same thing. All bad. I was writing myself off. *This is not looking good for you, champ.*

2

What I'd done

I was arrested on a Thursday. On the Wednesday I had quit my job, killed a man and set his body on fire.

I am not a good man. I have a temper and do not suffer fools lightly. Ever since I was a boy growing up in the outback of South Australia, I have held firm beliefs about right and wrong and have been unafraid to stand up for myself when challenged. I was raised to do things as well as they can possibly be done and took my counsel from the books and the thoughts that accompanied me during long hours alone as a boy in the desert. My dad was a cattle station overseer and a wildlife artist, and we would spend hours in the bush, not saying anything, me asking and answering questions in my head about why things were the way they were and what I could do to make them better. Having grown up in such isolation, I had rigid ideas about how men should be. When I was a teenager, this sometimes got me into trouble.

After I had been drawn into some fights and hauled up before a court in the remote South Australian town of Port Augusta, my mum told the magistrate that I was signing up for the Australian Army, which the magistrate accepted as a proper alternative to punishment by the law. During the fifteen years I then spent in the army, I guess I was known as someone who liked to do things his own way, was effective, and sometimes rubbed up against certain kinds of authority. I'd like to think that I was always dedicated to getting jobs done as well as possible, but others might have called me a maverick and a hothead. So be it.

I lost seven years of my life for a crime—murder—that I did not commit. I killed a man in self-defence. I was imprisoned for seven years because I never received a fair trial and was lied to and cut loose by the employer I trusted as a friend. If the lid was simmering before, during those years it popped right off. Every day was a battle to contain the anger inside me. The prison was a hell on earth, as I will attempt to show in these pages, but I'm afraid my words will never be up to the task of conveying the filth, the danger, the uncertainty, the noise, the stench, the hopelessness, the barbarity, the cheapness of life, the random violence, the anguish, and the sheer fucking boredom that I had to wade through day after day, more than two thousand days and nights, in what should have been my prime.

How did I survive? That's what this book is about, but be warned, the anger I felt every day was my best weapon in the daily battle for survival. Being fucked-off with my circumstances got me through a lot of dangerous situations. My constant anger made me scary to people who might have done me harm. The longer I was in prison in Afghanistan, the fewer hassles I had, because potential assailants were worried about what I might do. They might come to my cell and see me doing handstand push-ups or some other exercise in endless reps, and this would make them reconsider any plans they might have had to bother me. You don't come out of that experience and suddenly turn into the Dalai Lama. I had my own demons, but it was also anger that helped pull me out of my periods of depression and despair. I have written this book during my first year of freedom. Anger became my friend, and it still is. I feel that I owe it something. Will I seem like I want to settle scores with my enemies? What do you think got me out of bed when I was in jail, if not seething rage at the colleagues and treacherous 'friends' who betrayed me when they thought I couldn't hit back? This is how I survived seven years of mental torment and physical threat in the worst place on earth: anger and the desire for revenge. I might come across as filthy at the world and enraged from time to time, but this was my reality and I make no apology for it. My anger was not just a consequence of what I had been through. It also saved me. Anger was my armour.

That said, I have plenty of friends who say I'm actually quite a nice and surprisingly normal guy! And pretty much everyone, friend or foe, concedes that I am a straight talker. I have many flaws, but even those who took me to task or got on my wrong side would agree that I am honest, sometimes to my own detriment. I will tell my story as I remember it. I can't promise that my memory, with all that I went through, is one hundred per cent accurate, but I will be absolutely genuine in my recall of events. My account will be a thousand times more truthful than the shit that was pinned on me.

Since leaving the Australian Army in 2004, when I was thirty-two years old, I had worked as a private security contractor in Iraq, South Africa and, for the twelve months leading up to my arrest, for Four Horsemen in Afghanistan. Four Horsemen's founder, John Allen, was an American Special Forces veteran with whom I had established a good relationship. He was someone I trusted implicitly until Four Horsemen threw me under a bus.

The day before my arrest, in June 2009, John and his cadre of American managers were at the company's office in Dubai. In their absence, the guy in charge of Four Horsemen's Afghanistan office was Petar. In his mid-fifties, grey and balding, constantly smoking, Petar was one of the reasons I was quitting, so I took some pleasure that Wednesday in walking in and telling him I was resigning, effective immediately. There were a lot of reasons behind my decision, but the main one was that I felt my life was increasingly at risk due to the corruption and incompetence of the people I was working with.

Petar tried to talk me into staying. I doubt he really wanted me to, but he didn't want me leaving while John Allen was out of the country. 'Just stay till John gets back,' he pleaded.

One of the company's principal operations was convoy security—we looked after international, mostly American, truck convoys once they came out of Pakistan and travelled to Bagram Air Base and the other bases throughout Afghanistan. One of the US government's aims was to 'localise' security and transport logistics, transferring responsibility for providing trucks as well as guarding these convoys from their own military to private companies. In Iraq after the 2003 invasion, America had controlled such security, but when the USA's focus switched to Afghanistan, a decision was made to encourage the locals to build their own economy and maintain their own infrastructure. The Americans wanted inbound transport companies to be operated by Afghans, but the shortage of competent and honest local people meant that the companies had to be joint ventures, with Afghan ownership and manpower working alongside international managers and operators. My role was to lead Afghan security teams on convoy protection. For the company, it was lucrative thanks to the enormous amounts of American money washing through a barely regulated economy, but also extremely dangerous work, made more so because of the loose management arrangements between the private companies and the Afghans. In Four Horsemen's case, the Afghan side was led by Commander Haussedin and his Panjshiri militia. We were in bed with one of the most corrupt war lords in the country.

Here's a small detail of that corruption. The contents of the convoys we escorted around the country ranged from building materials to food and medical supplies to mail for American servicemen and women. These convoys contained the nuts and bolts of Afghan reconstruction after eight years of war and some things, like the mail, were deemed so important that if anyone threatened a mail convoy we were authorised to use lethal force. It was high-stakes business and you would think that every detail would be controlled strictly, but when the truck manifests—the lists of contents, numbers of trucks, numbers and size of containers—came in from the US military, Petar would simply cut and paste them into an email and pass them on, without checking what was actually in the trucks or how many trucks there were. At first I thought this was just Petar's gift for laziness and turning a blind eye, but during the time I worked at Four Horsemen, I discovered that it was actually a way of permitting things to be stolen from the convoys or, more often, added in. If you wanted to transport drugs or arms around Afghanistan, what safer way than to sneak them onto an American military convoy? And if the Afghan war lord responsible for moving those drugs and guns around was in league with the chief of operations of the security company, how easy would it be to just pay off that manager to refrain from checking what was in the convoys? I am not just speculating on this. I had seen it happen repeatedly over the previous twelve months, and I had done my best to stop it, but now I had to throw my hands up and go away to do something else with my life. Having struggled with many aspects of how Four Horsemen was doing things, I had developed my own separate Afghan teams, working as an outsider, getting into many firefights and ambushes while doing my very best to achieve a result. But the odds were stacked too heavily against me, and by June I just felt that I wasn't going to survive. We were getting shot at almost every time we went out with a convoy. My number was surely going to come up sooner or later.

I had been working on a fallback plan, a security company I was setting up with a former flatmate in Cape Town, Jon Goodman, who was also in Kabul doing security. I had a girlfriend, Belinda, with whom I wanted to start a new life in South Africa. By June 2009 I was ready to start that new life.

'No, I'm quitting, I'm leaving on a flight tomorrow,' I kept telling Petar. As the argument went around in circles, Anton came into Petar's office. Anton took Petar's side, appealing to our long-standing friendship to get me to stay. Anton was a Belgian whose parents had emigrated to South Africa, and I had met him in 2004. A very good martial artist, he had instructed me in unarmed combat on my Close Protection course in Cape Town. Anton had qualified as a paratrooper in the South African Defence Force but missed out on the Bush Wars, becoming active only at the end of the apartheid era. He had a few anger-management issues, however, including a tendency to get into physical confrontations. He was sent for counselling but the lessons failed to sink in and Anton soon got to the point where he couldn't earn enough to cover his debts. I did him a favour and talked Four Horsemen into hiring him over some of my other friends with far more experience. It was a mistake. Anton took out his frustrations on the Afghans he was working with, and after he had been out on the road on a few jobs, some of the Afghans came to me and said, 'We know he's your friend, which is why we're telling you, but we're going to kill him.' In Afghanistan, they have a different way of settling HR issues.

I went to John Allen and suggested, 'It might be a really good idea if Anton goes and works with Petar in ops.'

John said, 'Good call, that's what we'll do.'

Anton got a pay rise and went off the road, but falling in with Petar and others in the office only made things worse. When I'd first joined the company, I had spent time with this group but quickly grew tired of the long lunches filled with boasts about how they used to run around in the Balkan wars 'killing Muslims with hammers'. Big talkers, they weren't so keen on working. The easier, safer jobs they were up for, but anything out in dangerous territory they were not so keen on, and these were left to me and the Afghans. When we got into trouble and needed Petar's crew supporting us from the office, all too often they were out, or drunk and stoned. It wasn't a healthy clique for someone with Anton's issues to find himself among.

But here he was, taking Petar's place in trying to talk me around. He was calling on our now tenuous friendship to persuade me to withdraw my resignation: it wouldn't look good for them if they lost me while John Allen was out of the country. Petar flapped his arms and told me I should wait.

'After what happened yesterday,' I said, 'you really expect me to stay?'

This was the elephant in the room: I didn't trust these guys to ensure my safety, they knew it, and it had all blown up the previous day, the Tuesday.

For more than six months, I had been running my own security team, independently of the Macedonians and Panjshiris, with John Allen's blessing. We were doing the most dangerous jobs and getting involved in a lot of heavy contacts with insurgents, but before long I had noticed I was fighting on two fronts. When too many people knew where my convoy was going, we would get smacked time after time by ambushes, sometimes resulting in casualties. When I didn't tell the office what I was doing, we didn't get hit. That said something right there. In the end, I'd take the details and the timeframe in which I had to complete a job, then get it done without direct contact with the office. I informed only the US commands whose areas of responsibility I moved through and kept in direct contact with John Allen when he was around.

John had agreed to my request to recruit Michelle, an Australian colleague I'd worked with before, as my point of liaison in the office. Michelle had gone through the interview process and agreed to a salary, terms and conditions, but when she turned up to sign her contract she found out that she was not going to receive the negotiated salary. She confronted the new human resources manager, Cassandra, about this and found out that the financial controller, Tim, had decided she was getting too much and changed the contract. I listened quietly to all this, and told Cassandra that Michelle was entitled to the pay that had been previously negotiated. All of a sudden, Cassandra called security to get Michelle out. Trying not to laugh—this was so over the top it was funny—I asked Michelle to step outside while I tried to explain to Cassandra what was supposed to be happening. Cassandra reacted to this by promptly sending out an email to management saying that I had acted threateningly towards her and used my relationship with the company owner to benefit my friends.

It was not a major incident in itself, and was more than likely the result of miscommunication. But for me it was the final straw. I said to Anton, 'That's it, I'm out of here, consider this a verbal resignation. Pass it on to Petar and the boss, see you later.'

Within minutes, I had several emails from all the Ops people. I opened the first one from Anton—'Resignation not accepted' was the title—followed by all the reasons why I couldn't leave the company.

After leaving the office, I met up with Michelle and another friend, KC. I was living in the compound where the Four Horsemen office was, the standard Afghan arrangement of two-storey buildings with a walled exterior surrounding an internal courtyard. Most of the twenty or so expat employees of Four Horsemen lived there or in a series of buildings down the street, but Michelle was staying in a nearby compound, where KC, who was not employed by Four Horsemen, also lived.

While we ate lunch, I told them about quitting and we had a whinge session about how things were at Four Horsemen. I felt bad about bringing Michelle over and leaving her in it, but she could handle herself anywhere, and would probably do better in my absence. KC was supportive, as always. An ex-US Army Ranger, KC was a really cool kid and an outstanding medic who had won the Bronze Star and Purple

Heart in Iraq. During the war there, he had entered a building to drag out some injured soldiers and give them medical attention when someone dropped a grenade on him. He'd been lucky to survive and now had scars all over his back from the explosion.

From when we'd first met through mutual friends in Afghanistan, KC and I got on like embryo twins. He had come out on jobs with me and I had complete trust in him. He was also one of those gifted people who can do anything they put their minds to. He was learning to fly planes, he could parachute, and he was planning to study medicine and become a doctor. He had such an ear for languages, he picked up a workable Pashtun within three months of arriving in Afghanistan. He was amazing. Once when I went to Dubai with him, we were in a bar and he was speaking merrily with a group of Russian girls—in Russian. He'd only picked it up that night.

I told KC I'd had enough of Four Horsemen. My view is that if you're going to do a job, do a job. Money isn't a motivator for me and never was when I did private security work. I am totally, obsessively and sometimes unreasonably driven by doing a job the right way. I don't understand how people can take good money to do something half-arsed. KC had worked for another private security company and suggested we go to their compound and talk with them about future jobs if I became a free agent. He said there was something coming up in Somalia that I might be interested in.

While we were there, I received an urgent phone call. It was late in the afternoon by then, with the sun setting, and Four Horsemen had a convoy going out of Kabul to Ghazni, a city on the road to Kandahar about two hours south-west of Kabul. Part of the convoy was going to the American FOB

(Forward Operating Base, or military outpost) in Ghazni, while the rest of it was going to an air strip being built in the desert further south. Because of the nature of the operation, two Americans were with the convoy, and one of them, Richie, was calling me.

'We've been hit,' Richie said, 'and we can't get moving again.' I asked where they were, and he said they were still on the outskirts of Kabul.

'Where exactly?'

'It's the spot where there's a big creek line running through, where they sell the cattle during the day,' he said. 'Near the police station.'

I knew the spot—it was close to the ancient gate that marks one of the southern entrances to Kabul. There was a small police station to the side of a bridge crossing the creek. I asked Richie what had hit them.

'Well that's the weird thing,' he said. 'Half the convoy was over the bridge when an RPG [rocket-propelled grenade] was fired at us. But not really at us. It went over the top of us, and over the top of the police station.'

'So you weren't actually hit.'

'No, but the security guys won't let us start up again. We're just sitting ducks here.'

Although I had quit Four Horsemen a few hours earlier, I could not walk away from this. Everything about it sounded like a set-up. My immediate suspicion was that Richie and the other American on the convoy, Jimmy, were going to be kidnapped while the trucks were stalled. Their convoy's security was being managed by some Panjshiris employed by Four Horsemen—a bad sign. Even worse, the guy who had the crucial job of driving out ahead of a convoy to make sure the road was clear was a Panjshiri called Karim Abdullah.

'Karim Abdullah is telling us to stay put,' Richie said.

'Where is he?'

'He's with us.'

'With the convoy? Why is he with you?'

'I don't know, but he's telling us not to move.'

My suspicions went up a notch. If Karim Abdullah was doing that job, sure as shit something irregular was going on.

Karim had been working at the company since before I arrived in 2008. He was a road-watcher, a job that was crucial in convoy protection. We had used road-watchers in Iraq where, because the urban terrain in and around Baghdad was so complex and dangerous, we would send out four or five of them ahead of any job. They would be armed and equipped with radios, and would be in constant communication with us, describing the scene and assessing the threat. If you don't have good road-watchers, not to mention honest ones, you will probably be dead by the end of the day.

A critical part of the road-watcher's job was for him to stay separate from the convoy itself. If his car was identified as being connected with the convoy, then he was worse than useless: he was an advance signal to insurgents that a convoy was coming. So it worried me that Karim and his car were sitting with the trucks. Why was he with the convoy? And why was he holding them up, apparently stopping them from moving while it was getting dark and relatively safe?

I was a big advocate of running convoys at night. The insurgents in Afghanistan weren't well equipped for night attacks, and worked like everyone else: they did their job during the day, and went home to eat and sleep at night. I'd have had all convoys running at night, but most Afghans and also expats in the convoy protection business couldn't overcome their instinctive fear of the darkness. So they would operate in the day, and pay the Taliban not to attack them, or hire Taliban as guards—it was amazing how many Taliban worked as security contractors, receiving protection money. That's how it operated throughout the business, but it wasn't the way I worked. I ran my convoys at night, and didn't have to pay the enemy not to hit me.

When I finished with KC, I went back to the Four Horsemen compound, where Petar had been made aware that the convoy had been stalled on a bridge outside the gate to Kabul. He was happy that I'd come back, and took my reappearance as a sign that I had reconsidered my resignation. Far from it: I told him I was doing this out of a sense of responsibility to Richie and Jimmy. 'I'm not taking back my resignation,' I said. 'I'm just going out there to make sure everything is okay.'

'But Karim Abdullah is with them,' Petar said, as if this was meant to be a good thing. I just ignored him and went outside to get a car.

Petar liked using Karim Abdullah, as he was a tribesman of Commander Haussedin. There had been many convoys when Petar had said, 'It's safe for you to go ahead because Karim has been down there and he told us it's safe.'

But Karim Abdullah's presence was no guarantee of safety: in fact, more likely the opposite. In October 2008, I had just finished one convoy and was resting up in Ghazni, waiting for night to fall when Petar rang, asking me to escort two trucks back to Kabul as soon as possible for a mail run. He assured me Karim Abdullah had cleared the route and it was safe to move, so against my own standard operating procedures (SOPs), I set out. We got hit near Salar. Hard. Both trucks were destroyed, and we had casualties all round after four hours of fighting. Nevertheless, Karim Abdullah went back to the company the next day and said, 'There was no fighting.'

I wouldn't trust him or work with him after that. The Macedonians weren't happy with me, and assured John Allen that Karim was trustworthy and competent. I said to John, 'Okay, let me gather some evidence for you.' In December 2008, two months after the Salar incident, John permitted me to follow Karim on a job. I went out, keeping my distance behind him, when he was to scout a road on which a convoy was to follow. To my surprise—well, not at all—he didn't even bother to go and inspect the road. He just went home.

When I got back to the company, I said, 'Have you heard from Karim?'

Petar said he had phoned and said the road was safe.

'Bullshit,' I said. 'He just went home and rang you from there.'

Subsequent to that, a lot of emails passed between Petar and John about Karim. John had his suspicions, and was unsure if Karim was planning to participate in a kidnapping or set up a convoy for an ambush. John had said to me, 'If Karim acts up, you sort him out.' But John was not in the country a lot of the time, and Petar, as operations manager, reassured him that Karim was to be trusted. If John complied, and agreed to keep using Karim, it was possibly because he had to trust his own manager's judgement, but more, I believed, as part of keeping things smooth with Haussedin, who was pulling the strings. So many poor decisions were made because they were a choice between doing things Haussedin's way or facing the consequences of putting the war lord offside.

That said, I was irritated that Four Horsemen was still using Karim as a road-watcher in June 2009, and the fact that he was out with this stalled convoy, preventing it from moving on, only added to my sense that Richie and Jimmy were in serious danger.

The Panjshiris had a certain pattern of setting up a fake ambush, and I was convinced that this was happening with the convoy. They would station some of their people to shoot at a convoy their own Four Horsemen guys were protecting. As the Panjshiris were part of the Four Horsemen team, the shooters would not aim at the convoy itself, but fire over the top. They didn't want to hurt anyone. Then, their guys in Four Horsemen security would say to the westerners on the convoy—in this case, Richie and Jimmy—'It's not safe here for you, go back to the base, we'll handle it from here.' And then they would either stage another fake ambush to loot the convoy themselves, or bring in some extra trucks to transport what they wanted elsewhere under the convoy's protection.

These thoughts were going through my head as I set off with an interpreter and two Afghan guards from the company compound. We borrowed a white Toyota LandCruiser that belonged to one of the absent American managers. My own car, a heavily armoured and geared-up Toyota Surf (or Hilux), had already been taken by the convoy. I didn't like being in an unfamiliar vehicle, which added to my bad feeling about the whole day. Ever since late the previous year, I had set up my own sub-operation with my own guys, Pashtuns who were stationed in Ghazni, not Panjshiris from Haussedin's gang. My men were genuine fighters, some having come to us from the enemy side. I trusted them with my life and we ran our own race, with John Allen's blessing. But on this day I didn't have them and I didn't have my own car. I had a driver from the Four Horsemen compound, and two Panjshiri meatheads from house security, who felt like big men because they could hang out in Kabul with painted rifles pretending they were Americans.

I did at least have my own protective gear: body armour, helmet, Night Vision Goggles (NVGs), a Glock 19 pistol and an M4 rifle that I had built from spare parts and fitted with a suppressor and laser sights. It was necessary to source my own gear. On paper, the company had all the whizbang gear that the American military gave us as part of our contract, but in reality we were lucky if we got a couple of shitty AK–47s. The Americans gave Four Horsemen the budget for proper American firepower, but someone in the company pocketed that money. To equip us with AKs, Commander Haussedin used a relative who worked at the United Nations weapons decommissioning plant in Jalalabad. All captured weapons from the insurgency were sent there to be destroyed. But they weren't. Haussedin's relative signed papers saying that the weapons were gone, but they would resurface in the hands of Haussedin, were re-registered through the NDS, and were then sold back to foreign security companies such as Four Horsemen. A typical rort. The result was that our safety was compromised, firstly because most of the AKs were barely functional, having never been properly maintained, and secondly because people in firefights tend to focus on the weapon, not the person. American soldiers would identify enemy not by their uniform (as they didn't wear one) but by their weapons, and if they saw you with the distinctive curly magazine of the AK, you were putting yourself in danger.

I did invest a lot into decent weaponry and protection; you need to be able to select the right tools for the job. I even had one well-maintained AK that I took out when working low-profile. That mindset of independently taking care of my own weaponry and ammunition had saved my life many times in the past year.

As we drove, I was in and out of communications with Richie and Jimmy. In Afghanistan, the cellular communication towers were set up in a haphazard fashion so you needed several phones, some of which would be good in some areas but not others. I had four handsets on me, including a satellite phone. Richie told me that the convoy had got moving again in the meantime, 'but there's some weird shit going on here, because we're stalled again at Maidan Shar.' That was another hour along the road towards Ghazni and in a much more exposed place, out in the open desert, an extremely vulnerable location in which to stop moving.

When I arrived at the bridge where the convoy had initially been stopped, I got out of the LandCruiser to have a look. The situation was as strange as Richie had described it. The RPG had been fired more than a hundred metres over the top of the convoy, over the top of the police checkpoint, into a hillside where it had exploded harmlessly. The police, who were out and about, were unfussed. Clearly, the RPG had been fired without any intent to harm.

As I was looking around where the RPG had been fired from, wearing my NVGs because the light had fallen, I noticed something in the dirt. Having grown up in the bush and been a scout in the Australian Army, I know a little about tracking. I made out three sets of tracks: one in military boots and two in thongs. These must have come from whoever fired the RPG. What was strange was that for all the hours that the convoy had been stalled, there were no other tracks: nobody from the Panjshiri security team had even bothered to come out and have a look at where the RPG had been fired from. It was as if they knew there was no point.

We drove on to Maidan Shar, where the convoy was stalled. It was just before midnight when I got there. Maidan Shar itself was a small village, but the landscape where the trucks were sitting was very open. There was an American combat outpost near the town, staffed by no more than eighty or ninety troops, several kilometres from where the convoy was. Maidan Shar was literally on the edge of bandit country. We often stopped at the service station there to get fuel, sort out our trucks and take stock, making sure everyone was ready and alert to drive on to Ghazni. The next area was Salar—the word means 'rifle' in the local language—where I had been in so many fights it wasn't funny. Mostly, these weren't organised ambushes, but attacks from arseholes who would shoot at anyone who came through, for no real reason. That's Afghanistan.

I walked around and assessed the convoy itself. The forty trucks, carrying American building supplies and mail, were lined up along the roadside.

There was no moon, no light. A part of me was pleased to see that the drivers had turned their headlights off: the convoy was blacked out. Many Afghans are terrified of the dark, so they liked to leave all their truck lights on. But if you're a bad guy sneaking about, those lights are a gift. When I had started this job a year before, it had only taken me a few times of walking around a convoy smashing their headlights to get the message through to the drivers that they had to keep them off if they were stationary during the night.

The forty-odd drivers were milling about, smoking and talking, on the right-hand side of the road. On the left side were about the same number of Afghan security guys, nominally contracted by Four Horsemen but actually working for Commander Haussedin.

It didn't take me long to find Richie and Jimmy sitting in their car. After waiting in this spot for more than two hours, they were understandably frustrated. Another Four Horsemen guy, a Nepalese security guard called Chandra Singh Butt, was snoozing on the back seat.

'What the fuck's going on?' I said. 'Why aren't you moving?'

'Karim won't let the convoy move,' Richie said. 'He's saying stay firm.'

'You've got to get it moving and get on to Ghazni before the sun comes up,' I said. 'You don't want to be driving through Salar in the daytime. You'll get hit for sure.'

'We want to go,' Richie said, 'but Karim is telling all the Afghans that he's in charge and they're not allowed to move until morning.'

'What's he going on about?' I said. 'These trucks are pieces of shit. You stop them moving too long, you don't know if they're going to get going again.'

'They're not listening to us. I know we're technically in charge, but the one they're taking orders from is Karim.'

'Where is he?' I said.

They pointed to his car, a white Toyota Corolla about twenty metres away. Karim was sitting in the driver's seat and holding court, waving his pistol about and telling anyone who came up to him to go away.

Karim spoke no English, so I needed help understanding and communicating with him. I went to my driver, who acted as interpreter, and said, 'Go and tell Karim to stop fucking about. Tell him to go out, get ahead of the convoy like he's meant to do, and we'll get the trucks moving behind him.'

With my NVGs on, standing in the open doorway of our LandCruiser, I watched the terp go over. He said something to Karim, who replied tersely. In his early thirties, with a short beard and blue eyes, Karim was one of those men who thought that because he carried a pistol and was a Panjshiri with connections to the Americans, he was better than anyone else. You give some young men a pistol and a radio, they think they are a commander. The Panjshiris didn't wear body armour; they thought they were protected by their status. Karim's tribe dominated the secret police and covered up each other's crimes. No wonder they thought they ran the country. They did.

But now he was shoving the muzzle of his pistol in my poor interpreter's face and clearly telling him to fuck off. That was definitely not cool.

Afghans typically hated being the bearer of bad news. It was in the culture: better to hedge around the truth than say something that will displease the listener.

'Mister Rob,' the terp said shakily, 'he doesn't want to do that.'

He didn't realise that with my NVGs I had seen everything, including Karim threatening him with his pistol.

'You go back,' I said, 'and tell him that if he won't move, he can hand in his company identification card and weapons and fuck off home to Kabul. We don't need him.'

The terp went over, and again I saw Karim push his pistol into the terp's face.

A few moments later, the terp was back. 'Mister Rob. He says it's too dangerous, and you and the Americans should go back to Kabul.'

'You go back to him,' I said, 'and fucking tell him to move or go home.'

A definition of insanity is doing the same thing over and over and expecting a different result. I sent the terp back, without any hope that he could change Karim's mind. The same thing happened. I wasn't insane, I wasn't even angry, but I was out of patience. This was beyond a joke. My attitude was: if you don't want to do your job, fine, piss off. When the terp told me for a third time that Karim was refusing to move, I decided to go over and rough him up. There was no point speaking to him, as he wouldn't understand. I had to put on a show of temper so that he would get the message. This was the way I operated, both from my nature and through training. Coming up through the ranks of the Australian Army, I saw that the most effective NCOs (Non-Commissioned Officers) were those who could snap for a moment, deliver their message, and then cool down and move on. To the recipient, that was far more disconcerting and effective than an NCO who was perpetually angry. To discipline someone, you turn it on and turn it off. That's how my old man was when I was growing up, and that's how I am.

After the terp came back the third time, I slammed my car door and began stalking the twenty metres to Karim's car. I had my helmet on and my M4, with its suppressor fixed, slung across my shoulders. My NVGs were over my eyes, but I flicked them up just before I got to Karim.

There was no conversation. I reached in to grab him by the collar. I intended to drag him out of his car and maybe give him an open-handed slap on the head. That was all I was going to do. The stupid thing is, I shouldn't even have been there. Four Horsemen's problems weren't my problems anymore. But I cared for those two Americans—I had trained them up, they were my mates, and I was seriously worried that something bad was going to happen to them. So I did make it my own problem, for one last time.

As I grabbed Karim, he shoved his pistol into my face. I saw the muzzle come up. *Fuck.* I thought he was about to shoot me. I leaned back and jammed the M4 out on its sling. In less than a second, I rammed its muzzle into his chest and fired four rounds: *smack-smack*, pause, *smack-smack*. The way we'd been taught in the army. That was it.

I had no thoughts in my head but what to do next. My mind and body were consumed by the need to act. While still covering him with my gun, I stepped backwards and flipped on the torch mounted alongside the barrel. I took his pulse, but the light from my torch showed that he was obviously dead. I'd shot him in the middle of the chest, and a 5.56-calibre round at close range causes horrendous damage. I could smell the burnt propellant from the gun and the metallic, rusty scent of blood. Modern small arms ammunition travels so fast that when it hits the body's fluid cavities, it expands and throws out a mist of blood into the air. It looks like dust but it's blood, instantly atomised. As well as that, his body was pissing and shitting itself. When people die, there's nothing pretty about it. We're just animals at the end of the day.

I thought: *Karim Abdullah, you shouldn't have done that.*

I dragged him out of the car, took his weapon, and called the terp over to open the boot. He was the only witness who could have heard the shots—the suppressor reduces the sound of a 5.56mm round, pressed to a body like that, to barely louder than a hand clap—and nobody could have seen it. The night was pitch-black, Karim's car's lights were out, and everyone else was more than twenty metres away. At this point, the interpreter and I were the only ones who knew what had just happened.

Jimmy came over while I was still inspecting Karim with the light of my rifle. I didn't need to say anything. It was obvious. 'Right, we need to get moving,' I said.

Jimmy and the terp might have been in shock, but they did what I asked. When he opened the boot of the car, the terp indicated that there were packages. I went over and had a look. They were the size of coconuts, plastic bags wrapped with brown masking tape. Shit. The car was full of drugs. Whether it was heroin or hashish, I don't know because I didn't cut the packages open to look at them, but there was absolutely no doubt in my mind. Maybe part of Karim's plan for delaying the convoy was connected with this fairly large quantity of narcotics. I don't know; he wasn't in a position to tell me now.

I moved the packages aside to create some room. I picked Karim up, took his phone, and put him in the boot of his car. At first we couldn't close the boot, so we forced it down and shut it with some compression tape I had in my medical kit.

The next thing I did was call the company to tell them what had happened. Anton was the first one I spoke to. He didn't suggest any plan, but just freaked out and panicked. My emotions were calm. I had been in a lot of serious fights and had killed several enemy over the previous year, and was not feeling any anxiety over what I had done to Karim. He became an enemy when he pulled his pistol on me. I wished it hadn't come to that, but my state of mind at the time was, *What's done is done. What do I need to do next?*

Without any help coming from Anton, I tried to get in touch with some American Special Forces guys I knew at the FOB base in Ghazni. My plan was to take Karim's body to them and tell them what had happened. As our convoys were taking American military mail and supplies around the country, we had military status and to some degree were untouchable. Deaths such as Karim's, like others I had been involved in, were essentially regarded as combat fatalities.

I was confident that his death would be signed off by the US in this way. But that night, I wasn't able to get a response from those SF guys, and their base was obviously not the kind of place where you could just rock up at the front door with a bunch of Afghans, a dead body and a car full of drugs and say hi.

As we sorted through Karim's gear, Jimmy was saying, 'I love this fucking job.'

Just then, minutes after I had shot Karim, three guys turned up—one with an RPG launcher and two with AKs. The leader was a man called Anar Gul, a Pashtun who was ex-Taliban but aligned with Haussedin. Their RPG didn't have any rounds. It makes no sense to have a launcher and no rockets. Close by was a compound that had been used as a black prison by the Panjshiris, where Haussedin had a huge cache of weapons in a shipping container. I'd been taken there one night a year earlier to collect some guns and ammunition for the company. It was dodgy as fuck. But now it was very interesting to see these three guys turn up. I looked down at their feet. One guy was wearing military boots that our company had issued. Anar Gul and the other guy were wearing thongs. I was ninety per cent sure that they were the ones who had fired over the convoy and here they were, hanging around with the other Panjshiri security guys being paid by Four Horsemen to do, from what I could see, absolutely nothing.

Richie, who hadn't actually seen what I'd done but had joined the dots, came to Jimmy and me and saw us bundle the body into the boot. We left Richie with the convoy to escort it to Ghazni, and went ahead in two cars—the terp, the two Four Horsemen meatheads and myself in the LandCruiser tailing Karim's Toyota Corolla, in which were Chandra Butt driving, Jimmy in the passenger seat, and of course Karim in the boot.

We drove for more than an hour, with Karim's car in front of us so I could cover it. I made sure that somebody kept trying to call the American base, and I tried my contacts again, but it was hard to get through. Eventually, one of the team managed to speak to someone at the base, who agreed to let us in when we arrived with the body.

My plan seemed to be working until we ran out of darkness. I'd banked on being able to beat the rising sun to Ghazni. The Afghan police ran the checkpoints outside the town, and at night they were too shit-scared to come out; we could run straight through them. But once the sun was up, they would man their stations properly and block us from getting through.

Even though I had been awake now for more than twenty-four hours, I was thinking clearly. We had a car full of drugs and a dead body. Because of my employment by an American company, this would not be a problem at their base. But that meant nothing to the Afghan police at a checkpoint. If they pulled us over and opened the boot to find Karim and the drugs, it was not going to look good. The body we might be able to explain, but not the drugs.

I called Petar and told him the situation. All he could say was, 'This fucking, this fucking . . . this fucking . . .' The more he freaked, the more I found a little space of clarity.

'Right, Petar, this is what I'm going to do. I'm going to destroy Karim's car with whatever's in it. I'll take the body to the American base and leave it there. And then I'm getting out of the country.' I wasn't skipping the country to run away from the consequences of killing Karim, I was still proceeding with my existing plan of quitting Four Horsemen and going to South Africa to be with my girlfriend and start a new life, just as I had been going to do the previous day.

That was my plan. I wasn't going to let this stupid incident get in my way.

To hear someone speaking in complete sentences seemed to calm Petar down and make him compliant.

'Okay,' he said. Anton also came on the phone and agreed that this was the thing to do.

Looking back, there are so many things that seem more logical. One would have been able to just throw the drugs away on the side of the road in the countryside. And the body, for that matter. Problem solved. But the state of mind I was in, those solutions didn't even arise. I was still confident that we could get Karim's body signed off as a military death in an ambush and that there would be no serious consequences for me. The drugs were my concern, and I never considered just tossing them out the window. What made more sense was to consolidate ourselves into one car, dump and destroy Karim's Corolla with the drugs in it, and take the body through the police checkpoint before heading to the US base.

In the middle of nowhere, between Maidan Shar and Ghazni, we pulled over to the shoulder of the road. The sun was fully up now and there was always the chance of getting picked off by some early rising Taliban. In much of Afghanistan, it's not so implausible that a destroyed car would be found smouldering by the side of a country road. To Chandra Butt, I said, 'Tell the Afghans to get any stuff out of the car that ties it to the company.' We let off a few rounds into the dirt to make it sound to any neighbouring Afghans like the Corolla had got hit in a contact. One of the guys actually fired an expensive RPG round into the ground—what a waste.

While the others got to work on Karim's car, I busied myself with getting a thermite grenade out of the LandCruiser.

In retrospect, that order I issued to Chandra Butt haunts me. I never said, 'Get the body out of the car.' I said, 'Get any stuff out of the car that ties it to the company.' I should have been more specific in my command. It might have saved me seven years of shit.

The military had issued our company with thermite grenades, and these were one piece of ordnance that had actually made their way through. Called the AN/M14 Grenade, Incendiary, they are the size of a drink can, coloured bright red with black markings, and look like a smoke grenade. They do a lot more. Put one onto the engine block of a car, and it will burn a hole through that engine and everything around it.

I got one out of the LandCruiser and took it over to Karim's Corolla. I pulled the pin and put the grenade on the back seat. I walked back to the LandCruiser. By the time I arrived at our car, two things happened simultaneously: Karim's car went up in a ball of flames and it dawned on me that among the stuff we had taken out of his car, we had missed one thing.

'Where's the body?' I said. I looked at each of the guys.

Butt said, 'Oh, we thought . . .'

There was no time to point fingers. I'd incinerated the body in the car. This was more serious for me. Killing Karim had been self-defence so I didn't consider that to be a potential problem for me. But now, we—no, I—had destroyed the body, which would be found and identified with the car, and we were all witnesses to what would look like destroying the evidence to conceal something bad. Killing Karim was easily explained, but blowing him up inside his car was not. For the first time, I figured that I might be in some serious shit.

I could have gone off and yelled at the Afghans for being idiots, but I was taught never to show emotion in front of troops. The minute you start ranting and raving, they lose respect and get scared. It's always better to have a plan, even a bad plan, than run around like a headless chicken. I'd been in the battalion when leaders had lost their shit and everything went wrong from there. The army spends years on making good NCOs, drumming this into us. It's why we have such a good reputation overseas.

I got into the LandCruiser and told the driver to head for Ghazni. I thought, *Get me out of this country. What else am I going to fucking do?*

We punched on for another hour or so to Ghazni and waited outside the American FOB until the rest of our convoy turned up. I spoke to Richie and Jimmy together. Richie told us that the convoy had gone past Karim's burning car. Local police were already looking it over.

'Okay,' I said, 'here's what you've got to do. Finish the job. Then go straight back to Bagram, get out of the country and don't come back.'

It was a pretty short and simple conversation. The two Americans were my priority. If anyone came after me, I thought I could deal with it. They couldn't. As far as I knew, they did what I said and were out of Afghanistan quick smart.

By now, it had been the longest day. The previous morning, I'd woken up on the verge of deciding to leave Afghanistan. But it was to be on my terms: cutting my ties to this corrupt company and flying out to a better job and a new place. Another chapter, another adventure. Now, twenty-four sleepless hours later, as I drove back to Kabul with the interpreter and the Four Horsemen security pair, I was planning to leave the country in quite a different way and with a fair bit more at stake.

During that trip, I phoned Anton and Petar and told them we'd mistakenly destroyed Karim's body with the car. Even more urgently than before, I had to get on a plane.

It was mid-morning when we drove the LandCruiser into the Four Horsemen compound. I went straight to my room and began organising myself to leave. My passport and US$2000 in emergency money were on me at all times. I backed up all of my computer files and emails onto a separate cloud-based email account. I knew the company would go into self-protection mode and smash everything I owned, to cover their arses, and, for all I knew, I would be sacrificed. On that account, I was right not to trust them.

But I still didn't know which individuals I could count on. As I was packing my gear, a flustered Anton came into my room and said, 'The NDS are coming for you.' Could I believe him? It didn't matter. I had to assume the NDS were after me. Anton suggested I leave the compound and go to one of my friends' houses.

Without trusting Anton or anyone else enough to say where I was going, I went to the bank and withdrew $10,000 from my personal account. Then I went to Frank's compound to figure out my next step. I tossed my coin and decided on Kabul International rather than Bagram. Frank gave me some clean clothes to change into. I needed to sleep, but I was too amped up.

I made one phone call, to Belinda, in South Africa. She and I had met a little more than a year earlier, just as I was looking for a job in another country, as luck would have it. We had realised after a few months we might have a serious future together, but during my year in Afghanistan I had only got to see her once on leave. Over that time, we grew tired of being apart from each other and stressed from the long-distance phone relationship we had. I felt that if I wanted a future with B, I couldn't keep working in Afghanistan. I had finalised that decision the previous day. I was hoping to get back to South Africa to be with her as soon as possible.

But then I had made another decision, to go out to that convoy and help Richie and Jimmy, and one thing had led to another.

I told her what I'd done, and said I was hoping to get out in the next few hours. She was very upset, but promised she'd be waiting for me whenever I got to Cape Town.

Seeing Belinda—that was what I focused on as I walked out of Frank's place and got in the taxi to Kabul International. I figured that I would be seeing B within twenty-four hours.

3

On remand

For the three days after I was arrested, I disappeared into the Afghan prison system. If someone was going to murder me— the NDS, a crony of Haussedin's, some overzealous cop, an unhinged prisoner—now would be their time. Nobody knew where I was.

After the first night they moved me out of the cell with the living dead into another, where there were some Hazaras and one Nepalese man. We didn't communicate; I didn't know what they were in for. I spent all day crouched in a bundle, waiting, starving, vanishing into myself.

The serious beatings stopped for the main part, although cops, NDS or Haussedin's thugs would randomly show up now and then to give me a kicking. After another day, they moved me into a cell where I was on my own. I could actually walk around in small circles. It seemed like a big improvement.

I was in Tolkeef, the remand prison adjacent to the police headquarters in the centre of Kabul. Accused offenders of every kind were held there prior to their court hearings, but some would stay long-term, paying bribes even after they had been convicted, so that they could avoid being sent to the main prison, Pol-e-Charkhi, which was an hour or so outside the city. If it was worth paying money to stay here, the other place must have been horrific. I had no idea what Tolkeef looked like from the outside, as I'd been taken in a dark van from the airport. From the inside, it was an absolute fucking nightmare. The section of the prison I was in consisted of an open courtyard with alcove cells off it, patrolled by guards walking around on top of clay-brick walls that had been heavily damaged by earthquakes. There were close to 300 people in a space the size of a tennis court. Rotting garbage was stuffed into a concrete box in the middle of the courtyard, where a wood-burning stove poured out black smoke day and night that settled in the airless square. In the summer heat, the place reeked of decay. The cell I was put into, roughly three steps across, was insanely overcrowded, twelve people squashed together with their backs to the urine-coloured clay walls. The prisoners hung bags of possessions off wooden pegs they had stuck in the cracks in the brickwork. Guards brought in food once a day—rice, bread—but otherwise the prisoners were left to their own devices. There were no westerners and nobody I could speak to in English. I bundled myself into a ball and tried to disappear again. Every day I thought my future was more fucked up than the day before.

In this living hell, the days and nights blurred together. Prisoners did have contact with the outside; their friends or relatives were able to come to the chainlink fence on the outside border of the jail and pass them food. The prison system could never afford to feed its population, so it relied on families to make up the difference. Every day, that area was like a zoo, with visitors and prisoners literally climbing over each other to scream messages from one side of the fence to the other. As desperate as it was, this area of contact between prisoners and the outside world was my only hope that someone would find me.

During those first days, I didn't give much thought to Karim Abdullah. I wasn't bothered by what I'd done. I'm not a psycho, but with the benefit of hindsight I didn't think I would have acted any differently. He shoved his pistol into my face and I thought he was going to fire. About Karim personally, I felt no remorse. He was heading for a violent end one way or the other. If I hadn't killed him, one of his own people would have. What I did regret was forgetting to tell the Afghan security guys to get Karim's body out of the car. Already I figured that in the logic of the Afghan judicial system—if I made it that far—as a westerner, having killed a man would get me into trouble enough, but I could deal with that through the fact that I had acted in self-defence. Incinerating the body a couple of hours later would make it look much worse. Nobody would believe that it came about through a misunderstanding, and I could see it being used to paint a picture of the killing being intentional.

On the third day after my arrest, I was taken to an office in the police headquarters next door to the prison and was handcuffed to a chair. There were a couple of cops, and then in came Anton.

It should have been a relief that someone knew where I was, but Anton didn't offer me any reassurance. Nervous, grim and tight-lipped, he put a typed sheet of paper in front of me.

'Read what's here, then sign it, and sign a non-disclosure and disclaimer form,' he said. 'If you don't sign them, we can't help you.'

At first I wouldn't even look at it. I could imagine what it said: I was acting alone, I just drove down to Maidan Shar to shoot Karim on a whim, the company had nothing to do with it. There would be nothing about Anton and Petar begging me to stay with Four Horsemen and withdraw my resignation, and nothing about them giving me a company vehicle, equipment and staff to go out and check on a convoy the company was meant to protect. Nothing about them knowing what I'd done and agreeing with my plan to take Karim's body to the US base.

I said, 'You're meant to be my mate. What the fuck's going on?'

'I can't answer any questions.' Anton spoke as if we were strangers. He nodded towards the statement on the desk in front of me. 'This is what you've got to do.'

Eventually I read it. The statement left me holding the bag. There was no mention of Richie or Jimmy, the two Americans who had been at the shooting and, in Jimmy's case, at the incineration of the body. That meant they had probably been spirited out of the country, which was good, I guess, as that had been one of my objectives, but now it only made it easier for the company to isolate me. My 'confession', written by Four Horsemen, said that I wasn't working for them on the day of the shooting. I had resigned and was out there on my own. The statement said that the officials at the company had no idea what I was doing and no idea that I had taken their vehicle, driver and two security staff.

The main witness to the shooting, it emerged on the document, was Chandra Singh Butt, the Nepalese security guy employed by Four Horsemen. I said to Anton that they couldn't use any statement from Butt, due to the fact that he had been asleep in the back of one of the cars when the shooting took place. He might have been with me during the subsequent activities, but no way could he be a witness to the shooting. He never saw a thing. Four Horsemen's document also said that I had shot Karim with an AK47. I looked at Anton. This was complete bullshit.

'Just sign it,' he said wearily.

If this was in a first-world country, anyone could have seen how many holes were in the statement.

'Four Horsemen want me to go through the process and then drop me,' I said. Anton looked at the paper, his expression saying that he just wished I would sign it and let him get out of there.

With the cops standing around me, leaving no doubt about what would happen if I refused to do what was expected, I signed Anton's paper. I shouldn't have done it. But at the time, I had only one thread to hang onto, and that was my faith in John Allen's influence and in Four Horsemen. Remember, this was only three days after my arrest and I'd been through hell in Tolkeef. I thought that things could get no worse than this! If I did what Four Horsemen asked, I hoped they would look after me—meaning, they would pay the necessary bribes and get me out of the jail. I believed in Afghanistan's corruption so fully, I thought that if I signed this paper, somehow it would trigger the exchange of money to set me free within a day or so. I couldn't bear the thought of another week in jail—which was the worst I was still thinking would happen to me. I felt that my choice was between signing this bullshit confession and getting out within days, or not signing, going back to my cell, getting beaten up day after day, and being given up to the whims of the Afghan justice system. At the time, although I was caught between a rock and a hard place, I believed that to sign was going to get me out of there.

Anton left the office, and that was the last I ever saw of my old mate. I remain angry with him. Seven years in an Afghan prison don't teach you to be mellow and forgiving, and you don't come out wanting to shower blessings on all mankind. I would meet some rock-solid people during those years, and I would learn to appreciate goodness in surprising places, but it did not dissolve my anger against those who betrayed me. Prison bakes that anger into something hard and immovable. The anger becomes part of your core, it grows inside you and also around you, on your surface. This would also be a key to my survival. The white-hot anger I still feel towards people such as Anton and others helped to harden me and make me a dangerous person in jail, a person who could not be messed with.

When Anton went out of the office, his place was taken by a counter-terrorism policeman, a high-ranking one if the thickness of his epaulettes and the gold in his braiding were any guide. From his pale Eurasian look and his accent, I could tell that he was a Panjshiri—they were stacking up against me—and he put another piece of paper in front of me. It was all in Dari and I didn't understand a word of it.

'Now,' he said in English. 'You have to say yes to everything here or else you will be killed.'

Right, okay.

He read from the sheet.

'When you did this, were you working by yourself?'

'No, I was working for Four Horsemen.'

Without a pause, he went on: 'Did you intend to kill Karim Abdullah?'

'No, I shot him in self-defence.'

'You intended to kill him?'

'I'm not saying that, because it's not what happened. I shot him in self-defence.'

He looked at me and said, 'That's not what it says in your statement.'

I was in no doubt that, in the hands of the counter-terrorism police, if I did not sign this statement they would beat me to death. So, once again, without any representation, under complete intimidation and coercion, I signed.

I was in the darkest despair. I didn't trust a soul in this country, not one fucking person.

———

Somehow, during that next week, KC found me. Having found out where I was, he worked his way through the system and came to the prison with some money and a handful of Snickers bars. We talked through one of the gaps in the prison wall, a total space the size of an upright single bed, covered in wire. I was struggling among a mass of Afghan prisoners, all trying to communicate with their friends on the other side of that slot. KC, battling with a similar-sized group on his side, looked worried, but he was very on-task, the Ranger in him coming out.

'How did you find me?' I shouted.

KC smiled. 'I speak Pashtun, remember? I have my ways.'

He was only there for fifteen or twenty minutes, but KC saved my life, by finding me and bringing me food and, equally importantly, by then contacting the Australian embassy in Kabul to tell them about my situation. Once he said he would inform the embassy of where I was, I began to believe that

I might not vanish. About four days after KC's visit, that hope turned to a limited kind of joy when I was taken to a visiting room in the eight-storey office block next to the jail.

Sitting at a long table was one of the staff from the embassy. Leanne was clearly efficient. In her late thirties, medium height with curly hair and glasses, she was serious and to the point. Comforting as it was, the sight of Leanne was not what gave me the biggest boost. Next to her was the head of the embassy's security contract, a huge man-mountain with sandy brown hair, a little older than me.

'Ivan?' I said. 'I didn't even know you were in country.'

Sometimes providence sends you a sign. It sent me one of my oldest mates from 1st Battalion Royal Australian Regiment [1RAR] in the Australian Army. Ivan and I had been diggers together, in the same section in the same battalion, way back in the early '90s. Within the army, it was all a matter of finding like-minded souls. From my bush upbringing, I'd gone to Kapooka thinking the army would be awesome and everyone would see things the way I did: they would be serious about training and doing things the right way. Imagine my surprise when I realised what it was really like. There are some people who can only survive inside a strict institution, who would be hopeless anywhere else, and a lot of people were like that, only there for the pay cheque. Then there were a minority, probably only twenty per cent, who truly believed in what they were doing. I wished the whole army was like that. Then again, at the time, there were no wars on and the digger of today knows exactly what he's getting into by going to an infantry battalion. Wars seem to bring reality home for command structures and training establishments alike, and the Australian Defence Force as a whole is better for it.

From Kapooka I went to Singleton in New South Wales for more training, and then to the 1RAR in Townsville, proud to be part of what was reputed, and what I believe, to be the superior battalion in the Infantry Corps. Other battalions would call us a bunch of arrogant arseholes. That reputation has always been there, even among the older diggers: 1RAR think they're better. More guys go to specialist units from 1RAR than anywhere else, and it has a reputation for producing people who end up doing something. People who want to get things done and not back down. And also some who end up in jail for doing stupid shit.

When I started at Townsville I found a group of like-minded mates, including Blaine Diddams—an absolute champion who, after years in the SASR, would be killed by Afghan insurgents in 2012—and we stayed in for the long run together. It was a good job and a good lifestyle, and those friends became as close as family. If you asked them what I was like in the battalion, the answer would be 'good in the bush, pisswreck in barracks'. Barracks life can be boring and I got myself in some trouble on occasion, usually seeing how far I could push things, usually for my own entertainment.

One day, for example, our lines, or barracks, were being inspected by our company commander, with everyone standing at attention by our made beds in our rooms. The officers had a quick look at mine and then moved on to the next room. Then the senior NCOs came through. This is where arses get kicked and the next lot of duties get filled. The company sergeant major (CSM) came in, had a look around, checked my balcony, then said, 'What's that, Private Langdon?'

He was looking at the ceiling. I followed his eyes up. Stuck to the ceiling above our heads was a VB carton from the previous night.

'It's a VB carton, sir,' I said.

'And what's it doing up there?'

'I'd be in the shit if I left it on the floor, sir,' I said.

'Who's your fucking section commander?'

Didds was watching the entire exchange across the hallway, silently pissing himself with laughter. I'm pretty sure he had convinced me, at some point, that fixing the carton to the ceiling was a good idea. Needless to say, I did a few formal guards the next duties week.

When Ivan came to the battalion, in 1991, it was an off-pay week. Didds and I were broke as usual, hanging out for the next week to roll around, but Ivan, fresh from the School of Infantry, had money, so we took him out on the piss in Townsville. Funny how one night out can set the standard for a friendship.

We all worked in the same platoon in 1RAR for years and remained friends after Iran and Didds applied for SASR selection and got in. By the early 2000s, while Didds stayed in the SASR, Ivan left the army altogether and went into private security contracting. We had worked together during my four years in Iraq, and he was always someone I could rely on for honest advice. Ivan could be like the Sphinx, giant and silent, but he was extremely intelligent and could persuade people to do what he wanted. As a project manager on jobs, he had the perfect balance of being able to keep both the clients and the workers happy—a task that is much harder than it sounds.

I was a wreck of a human when Ivan and Leanne found me in Tolkeef. Our first meeting did no more than cover the basics. Leanne told me that the embassy could keep track of me and ensure that I wasn't being mistreated, but not intervene in my legal case. I had more urgent needs. I was suffering from gastro, and Leanne said she and Ivan could bring tablets to help with that and any other minor ailments. She also had some books and magazines that she handed over immediately. I was just grateful that they knew I was there. From that moment, my fears that I would be killed in a random beating and thrown in a pit without anyone knowing began to ease. A little.

I still didn't know what was going to happen next. I had asked for a lawyer, but no one had been assigned and I didn't even know the process. The prison police barked at me in Dari and I didn't know what was going on, though I assumed there was a court date coming up. Leanne told me that she would try to clarify the process, but there were days to wait and burrow into my little shell before her next visit. In those first weeks, she came once every three days, bringing bottled water, medicines, books and magazines, plus water purification tablets so that I could drink from the taps in the courtyard. She gave me access to a phone, on which I could call my sister Katie and discuss what to do next. That was great, although Katie was still being told by Anton that Four Horsemen was going to take care of me. That aside, there were strict limits to what Leanne could do. She always repeated the same bleak information that the embassy could not intervene in my case. She eventually got her arse kicked by her superiors in the Department of Foreign Affairs and Trade (DFAT) for coming to visit too often, but she was the first of several staff members of the embassy who went above and beyond the call of duty to be compassionate and helpful.

I did nothing in those first days in Tolkeef—no exercise, no conversation, just tucked myself into a ball and tried to disappear. I remember few details of the place because I spent hour after hour on the floor with my face lowered onto my knees. It wasn't like I could take a wander and check the place out or get my bearings. I had no idea who else was in there or for what. I just closed my eyes and shut my brain down. When I needed to go to the toilet, in a disgusting non-functioning room down the hallway, I would pick my way over the sleeping bodies. These walks were my only exercise, but they exposed me to more horrors. I remember a guy with Down syndrome who was chained up by his neck to the wall near the toilets. A bunch of prisoners was standing around throwing things at him—water, rubbish—or poking him with broom-sticks. They screamed at him for entertainment. It sucked the fucking soul out of you, made you hate people. The author-ities were just dumping disabled people here because there was nothing they could do about them. I saw it a lot over the years, the use of prison as a disposal unit for humans. 'Why is he in jail?' I asked guards or prisoners from time to time. 'He's crazy,' they would say. As if that explained it.

KC came two or three more times over the next week, bringing me food and money. He and I crammed up on both sides of that hole in the wall until he was able to talk his way past the guards and come at a time when rent-a-crowd wasn't also fighting to talk through the fence. But on his last visit, he said, 'Sorry, man, I've got to bail.' KC had worked for a company owned by another friend of mine called Marcus Wilson. When Four Horsemen needed extra medics to work with their convoy protection teams, they subcontracted to Marcus's crew. This arrangement was still ongoing at the time of my arrest, and KC said he couldn't keep visiting me because someone at Four Horsemen had told him, 'If you don't stop going and seeing Rob, we're going to kill you.'

I said, 'Okay, I know what they can do. That's cool, mate. Thanks for everything.' We were both gutted, but there wasn't much else we could say.

After KC's last visit, Marcus came and saw me. We had a close bond. Marcus had been with me on what had been a life-changing mission a few months before, to rescue a burnt Afghan girl by helicopter from Khost, near the Pakistan border. As a western medic, Marcus drove up to Tolkeef in his ambulance and told the prison authorities that he wanted to come in and treat me. As a bribe, he gave them a few Panadols, and they let him in. He gave me shots for cholera, typhoid, polio, tuberculosis and the other illnesses that were rife in the jail. Needless to say, I was coming down sick. Afghans generally have a different concept of personal space anyway and prisoners who were obviously contagious would cough right in your face. The wake-up alarm each morning was someone hawking up phlegm in his throat, and that noise of someone hawking still chills me more than the sound of keys jangling or iron doors slamming. Marcus would keep visiting me over the next three years, taking care of my medical needs. Luckily, I never contracted any serious illness, but I often felt lousy with flu and diarrhoea that rarely got critical but never seemed to leave my body completely.

I didn't tell Marcus what KC had told me about why he couldn't come anymore. There were people at Four Horsemen, most of all Commander Haussedin, who played for keeps, and I didn't want to put anyone in danger. As I sat in jail and pieced things together, a lot of my thinking was focused on Four Horsemen and what they had done. I was still trying to figure out who I could trust. I had assumed, from the beginning, that it was the Macedonians who had turned me in. The Panjshiris who were with me when we burnt the car would have told Commander Haussedin, and he would have been after me from the start. We had a history of antagonism and he would have relished any opportunity to get me.

But he wouldn't have known exactly when I was going to the airport, and that I was going to Kabul International rather than Bagram: it was Petar and Anton who knew that. When the police at the airport came to arrest me, they had had my company ID photo and my passport details. There was only one place they could have got that: the company. When Anton had spoken to me that day, he knew that the police were on my trail. I wondered now if he was keeping tabs on me so that they would know exactly where to get me. It's possible. Of the people in the company only Elena, Petar's wife, had shown me any loyalty, by giving me that urgent warning.

Anton's complicity was reinforced by his behaviour when he came to the jail and made me sign the statement exonerating the company of any responsibility. I began to join the dots. There was also the company's threat against KC to stop seeing me. What kind of people had I been working with for the past year? Were they even worse than I'd suspected? Had there been an organised conspiracy among them, Haussedin and the police to stop me from leaving the country?

Even though I had been found by Ivan and the embassy, I was in a desperately isolated and vulnerable position. When it came to Four Horsemen, I had to assume that I was truly on my own now.

4

LEFT FOR DEAD

'If you ever find yourself in the shit,' an older and much wiser friend once told me, 'make sure you keep your watch—it's an escape kit on your wrist.'

Once I'd been discovered by Leanne and Ivan and felt a bit safer—at least I wasn't going to be mysteriously 'disappeared' now that they had eyes on me—I began to grasp at alternative plans to get out. In my first days in jail, there was always a new theory, like get-rich-quick schemes. I kept hoping that a miracle was about to happen. In the security industry, one of the most widely acknowledged wearable escape kits was a Rolex watch, which could be as good as gold, literally. It was widely believed that if ever you needed to pay someone a bribe to get out of jail, you only needed to hand over your watch. I had a Rolex, worth six or seven thousand US dollars. Worth my freedom, maybe. But it was actually worth nothing. Like the twelve grand I had on me when I was placed under arrest, the Rolex had been stolen. I had left it with my gear back at the compound, and someone nicked it. My escape kit had escaped.

This was actually the beginning of a litany of pilfering, by people known and unknown, so that by the time I got out of prison I had lost almost everything I owned. Some of it went on open bribes, some of it went on legal fees, and some of it just . . . went.

The initial problem was that, being in prison, I was given up for dead. At my home at the Four Horsemen compound, I had left a lot of personal valuables, including the Rolex. What was eventually returned to me, out of all those effects, was a small container that looked more like a lost property box: odd socks, a single shoe that had lost its partner, a shirt that I'd never seen before. Out of sight, I was seen as fair game.

I got a visit during my first few weeks in Tolkeef from Jon Goodman, my South African ex-flatmate with whom I'd been planning to start up a security company. Jon had come from a tough background, taking care of his mother and siblings after his father walked out on the family. He was a police reservist in South Africa but was not as experienced as a security contractor. Another mate of mine in Cape Town and I had put in a good word for him at Global, one of the other companies in Kabul, so he got a guernsey. Guys I knew from 1RAR started calling or emailing me saying, 'Who is this fucking idiot? He a mate of yours?' I'd stick up for him, saying he just had a tough upbringing, that he just needed some experience. After a few years he moved to another Global contract, ironically protecting the US specialists teaching the Afghans how to run their prisons. There were more South Africans on that job, so he got on better there.

Earlier in our friendship I had invested a substantial amount of money with him in setting up a new security business in South Africa. My ultimate plan was to build up my savings in Afghanistan and then return to South Africa to help run that. When I got arrested, Jon visited me in Tolkeef to check up on my welfare. The last thing I said to him on that visit was, 'Help Belinda out if she needs it back in Cape Town. If she comes over here, make sure she's safe and check up on where she ends up staying.'

'No problem, brother, I'll do what I can,' he told me.

When Belinda did come, she filled me in on what had happened back in Cape Town. She had emailed Jon asking for help with a few things, like getting the rest of my gear and sorting out what was going to happen with the assets in the company. The tone of Jon's reply email was smug and almost vicious. He told her there were no assets left and she should never contact him again. Eventually she managed to get some of my stuff back with the help of another friend of mine. It's funny how the possibility of a sudden windfall can make people change, but maybe with Jon it was there all along. Maybe he was more like his father and hid it under a mask. Maybe he only came to see me to make sure that I wasn't getting out in a hurry. I still look at those emails whenever I think I'm being too trusting with someone.

I was easy prey, caught between those primal emotions, hope and fear—hope that some miracle might spring me free, and fear that my hope would lead me down desperate and naïve paths that led to me getting ripped off. Hope was the more dangerous of the emotions, because it led me into alliances with some very dubious characters. It took years before my hope would evaporate, but once it went, so would my fear.

A few days after the arrest, I was huddled in my cell in Tolkeef when I heard a voice in the courtyard outside the door speaking English with an Australian accent. This guy was blowing up at the guards because he had military-style boots with laces, and the guards wanted to take them off him. I went out and saw a man, about ten years older than me, short-haired and clean shaven but for a soul patch on his chin. We stood out from the crowd as the only two westerners. We made eye contact.

I said, 'Are you from the embassy?'

His name was Glen, and he was a fellow prisoner. 'I've been arrested because I've got an Afghan wife and I'm not a Muslim,' he said. 'I've broken the law because I didn't convert.'

I was a bit dismissive at first. 'Dude,' I said, 'I've got bigger problems to deal with. But you've got to lose the boots.'

'*You're* allowed to keep *your* boots,' he complained, pointing to my Blundstones.

'Yeah, but that's because they don't have laces. It's the laces they don't want you to have.'

If there was one constant about the Tolkeef prison, it was that it denied you the alternative to go off and be alone. You could only escape the constant din and crush of people by finding somewhere with different people. There was no solitude. Glen, who seemed like a nice guy, was the first inmate I didn't want to get away from. Soon we were talking, passing the time by swapping stories about our common experiences. He liked some of my exploits so much that they ended up in a book he wrote after his release, turned into stories in which he was the main character. I guess that's a form of flattery? He actually dedicated his book to 'Rob, to whom I owe my life'. Well, that suggests we were a lot closer than we were, and I certainly didn't save his life. Glen would be in jail for three months. I was there for a lot longer, counting the cost of what he took from me.

Glen had some military experience—albeit in the Army Reserve—but we knew some of the same people, and we had both worked in private security for Edinburgh International, who had been my employers for nearly four years in Iraq. Glen and I had actually met before in Afghanistan. He didn't recognise me, but I remembered him as one of a group I'd come across while they were out on the piss in Kabul.

Glen's Afghanistan problems had started when an American called Deborah Rodriguez published a book in 2007 called *Kabul Beauty School*, about her teaching hairdressing skills to Afghan women to give them financial independence. She set the women up in her home for protection where she lived with her husband Samer, who worked for the all-powerful Afghan war lord Abdul Rashid Dostum— a complete psychopath with whom I had briefly crossed paths while I was working as John Allen's bodyguard.

In Deborah Rodriguez's book, there was a Hazara girl called Zara, who received death threats after its publication. Deborah hired Glen to take Zara to India for her safety, but along the way he got her pregnant. She had the baby, and they moved back to Kandahar, where he began working as a security contractor. He told me that he'd been arrested for breaking a law that stopped westerners from marrying Afghans, and that Zara had also been arrested for marrying an infidel. Zara was also a Shia Muslim, which put her at odds with the majority Sunni sect in Afghanistan. She and their three-year-old son were being held in a women's jail in Kabul. To try to avoid the possibility of being hanged and also to get out, Glen converted to Islam immediately when he entered the prison, under the guidance of a Taliban mullah or religious expert, but while his conversion had saved him from the death penalty, it had not been enough to get him, Zara and their child out.

Leanne from the embassy was turning up every couple of days. She was very switched on, as always, and gave a fair hearing to Glen, who told his story when she came and interviewed us both. He was in tears about his wife and son. It was a touching story, and I felt genuinely sorry for him. What a barbaric place it was, where a whole family could get thrown into jail for being the wrong religion, and kept there even when the conversion had taken place. After his own quick conversion, Glen said his wife was converting from Shia to Sunni in the other jail. I promised to do what I could to help him, and he promised the same to me. We began to look out for each other.

One way to team up was in getting hold of a phone. There was a Pakistani businessman in the cell, Faheem, who spoke good English and had a cheap Nokia phone, which he was using constantly to sort out his own release. For no cost, he lent the phone to Glen and me to make calls out. These calls were not approved by the guards, so Glen would stand and play lookout while I was on the phone, and I did the same for him.

The first person I called on that phone was my sister Katie. She and I had been close growing up, which was not unusual considering how few other kids we knew. Katie was two years younger than me, and for about ten years we lived on Billa Kalina Station, a South Australian cattle property near Lake Torrens, hundreds of kilometres north of Adelaide. The nearest towns were Roxby Downs, where uranium was mined, and the opal mining towns of Coober Pedy and Andamooka. Katie, myself and the two children of the station owners, who were a similar age to us, were essentially home schooled, with half an hour a day spent on School of the Air—a radio link to a teacher in Port Augusta with the classroom spread out over the entire state. At age twelve, I went away to board with a family and go to high school at Woomera, a town that had started out as a joint UK/Australian weapons testing facility but in the '80s had become a US Air Force base, part of the American satellite monitoring network. A few years later, when Katie began high school, our entire family moved to Port Augusta and I stayed there until I joined the army.

Katie and I had stayed close all the way through my travels, even though she had never set foot outside Australia. In 2006, after she gave birth to her first daughter Maddie, she phoned me in South Africa. She was really upset and was saying, 'She's died, she's died.' I got straight onto a plane and was back at Port Augusta within two days. When I turned up, a funeral was about to take place—but it wasn't Maddie's. It was our grandmother, who was in her nineties, who had passed away. Everyone was a bit surprised that I'd shown up so urgently. I loved my grandmother, of course, but the real reason I'd dropped everything and flown home was that I'd misunderstood the phone call. Family members still tell the story to show how close Katie and I are, but also how sometimes the detail gets lost amid the emotion!

When I got hold of Katie on Faheem's phone, I told her exactly what had happened and why I was in prison. Katie already knew, after Belinda had called her directly, and had since had conversations with DFAT. Anton at Four Horsemen had also told Belinda he was in touch with Katie and DFAT, and at that point, Belinda still believed him. Only after not hearing back from Anton did Belinda ring Katie and find out what the real story was—Four Horsemen was trying to cut all communication between people who knew me. DFAT only found out through KC. Katie and Belinda talked to each other regularly after that, and their combined efforts added some pressure onto Four Horsemen. Soon after, they began to send some food to me every few days.

The emotional tone of our first calls was matter-of-fact and practical. Katie was quite composed. In our family, we don't let things get to us when they're going pear-shaped. Dad has always been taciturn. Having done an apprentice-ship as an electrician at his mother's insistence, he never worked in that job for a day and instead went bush as a station overseer. He would work on cattle and sheep stations right into his seventies, training dogs to round up stock, but his real love was the bush and its wildlife: he turned himself into a very talented and proficient artist, sketching and painting the birds he came across in the bush. Dad was always working, and when he wasn't, he was out doing his own thing, observing and drawing birds, or sketching tree branches and bushes for his paintings, making sure the birds were always in the right ones. We always got on, but temper-amentally I was like him, enjoying being alone and doing my own thing.

My mum came from a military family. Her father was in the Royal Australian Navy in World War II, both her sisters were in the Navy and she herself was in the Air Force for a while. It was always on the cards that I'd spend some time in the military. Mum did jobs around the station while

Katie and I were small, but later she became a teacher's aide, working first at School of the Air, then later with disabled kids, and she would continue in that job into her sixties.

My first conversation with Katie from jail was quite businesslike, without histrionics: here's the problem, how do we move forward, just get stuff done. Anger doesn't solve anything and getting emotional doesn't either. Later maybe, but not on the spot.

I asked Katie to keep the news under wraps from our parents. They were quite elderly by now, and Dad had suffered from depression for a few years. I didn't want to upset or worry him and Mum. Of course, in my head, I was going to get out of prison before they even knew I'd been in. (I didn't know this, but Katie had told Mum and Dad straight away.)

Katie asked if there was anything else. I gave her my email password and said, 'Get everything out of my account, copy it, keep hold of it somewhere, and change the password. Once you've read it, you'll understand why. You'll know that I'm in the right.' I had to assure her that the incident wasn't just me losing my temper one night. Once she saw all the emails and files that I had from my time with Four Horsemen, she would see how much corruption was swirling around my arrest and how dirty the whole business was. On the downside, once she read this stuff and kept it safe, she began shitting herself because she didn't know if someone from the company would turn up on her doorstep.

Now that Belinda knew, she immediately began making plans to come to Afghanistan to see me. I still believed I was going to be able to get out before her trip was necessary.

Faheem, the Pakistani, was released within weeks, so Glen and I had to find other ways of making things work for us. As usual, it involved money. I had received small amounts of cash from KC and Ivan, but it soon went. We had to pay for the hot water boiled in stoves outside the cell. We had to pay for food of any substance: from the Afghans we got bowls of rice with a stew of oil and gristle. When Glen ran out of money, I shared my food with him because nobody else would. After Faheem left, other prisoners who had phones would charge us to use them. Then, while we were on a call, the prisoners told the guards, who would come in and catch us. If we did not pay a further bribe, they threatened to send us to the notorious punishment wing of Pol-e-Charkhi prison, the big jail outside Kabul we'd heard nightmarish stories about. Glen got caught twice on the phone and I got caught once; we both paid up. The fine could be anything from a hundred to five hundred bucks.

When it came to a haircut, we had to pay *not* to have the service performed. There was no regulation that required we have our hair cut; the guards just did it to fuck us off. More than likely this was a leftover from the Russian days: another step in the process of dehumanising the prisoners. I couldn't be bothered shelling out more cash to keep my hair, so we were sat down on straw mats while an old guy ran his rusty electric clippers over our heads. Glen ended up handing over a few notes in Afghan currency anyway. Soon after, our clothes were taken away and replaced by a prison 'uniform', a set of white flannelette pyjamas with upside-down scales of justice printed on them, some kind of statement designed to show how organised the authorities were when we would eventually show up in court. The uniform reminded me of the PJs we used to have as fresh army recruits at Kapooka, which we had to fold into perfect squares for inspection.

Tolkeef was a dangerous place when it came to sexual assault, but it didn't affect me personally. Every Thursday night, the police would come in with a gang of little 'shooter boys', gay prostitutes they had rounded up off the streets. The cops would leave them in the jail for three nights and let them go on Sundays. The jail was packed for those three nights. Some of the shooter boys saw it as a business opportunity, while others were abused quite horribly by both the cops and the prisoners. When I asked Faheem or the others about this practice, they would say, 'This is allowed in Islam.' I tried to blot it out. It had nothing to do with me. I just tried to make myself invisible until I was out of there.

I made some connections with other prisoners and did my best to help them. There was another non-Afghan in our section at Tolkeef, a Nepalese man called Rai who had been in there for two years. He was refusing to pay a bribe that would have released him. I ended up paying it for him, but a year or so later, when I was in Pol-e-Charkhi, I was frustrated to see him reappear. Rai was a cool guy, but was too stupid to leave the country when he'd had the chance.

Glen, my fellow Aussie, was the guy I really wanted to help. He was shitting himself, both literally and figuratively. Gastro was scouring both of us, and he was not coping. After his conversion to Islam, he was trying to nail down his religious learnings. He would pace around for hour after hour trying to memorise the account he planned to tell in court. The longer we were in there, the more sympathetic I became when I thought of his child. Sticking a three-year-old in a place like this was worse than cruel: the imprisonment, malnutrition and lack of safety could destroy a young child's future.

Glen had some interesting associates, one of whom was also in the prison. Alex was an Afghan who grew up in America before he was deported back to his home country after 9/11. He owned a nightclub and dealt drugs in Kabul, and his association with Glen was complicated and very different to the story Glen had initially told me about why he was in jail. Clearly there was more to Glen's background than I knew, but I still gave him the benefit of the doubt. It wasn't a place where you made judgements about people. You had to think practically about how you could help each other, and be pragmatic rather than emotional. For example, Glen told me he wanted to kill Alex, but he changed his mind when Alex said he could help us move into a 'VIP room', a section of Tolkeef where it was quieter and the cells had bunks and their own cooking area.

Glen and I accepted the offer and paid a further bribe to go into the room. I paid Glen's share. This was the VIP room, but there were no luxuries about it. It was in a different section of the jail, built for six hundred people but stacked with more than a thousand. There was a big square with a corridor around it and rooms off that. In one corner of the square was a mosque, and in another corner was one guy who had set himself up as a launderer alongside another who was boiling water. The yard was full of water overflowing from the laundry and sewage, and smelt of cigarette smoke and rotting garbage. Along the corridor there were three lots of showers and toilets, none of which worked, and cells built to hold six to eight people but which usually had fourteen or fifteen living in them. I didn't exercise at all, or even move very much. The guards would do a count every day that took hours, and you couldn't move while that was going on. I spent nearly all of my time on my arse. Room 1, where we ended up, had a fan and a 'servant' prisoner working for the inmates, doing the cooking. The floor was covered in blue-grey plastic carpet, the walls were painted grey, and outside light came in through a high strip of heavily barred windows. The stink of sewage from the toilets wafted everywhere and permeated every corner. The noise was constant—people babbling non-stop in Dari, Pashto and Urdu. The talking was like white noise, it was so constant, all night and day except for prayer times when we got some peace. To avoid people, I only left the room to walk around in the courtyard when it was the evening mealtime and the other prisoners were sitting and eating, or curled up on the floor trying to sleep.

Still, the VIP room was better than where we had been. Glen took the one available steel-framed bunk while I chose to sleep on the floor. In the bunk above Glen was the mullah who was helping him with his conversion to Islam. But our first stay didn't last long. An Afghan prisoner took exception to our getting 'favourable treatment', whatever he thought that was, and got into a wrestling match with Glen. I don't know what Glen did specifically to provoke the Afghan prisoner, but they were tussling like animals and I had to break them up. The police came in, blamed Glen and me for starting it, and kicked us out of the VIP room into a concrete hallway where we had to sleep in the only unoccupied space, in a stream of sewage-filled water flowing out of the toilets. Even the Afghans put scarves over their faces to avoid the stench. The toilet itself was a hole in the floor, and the walls were covered in shit from where the locals had wiped their hands. The toilet was always overflowing and the Afghans would keep shitting on it, so it piled up. If it piled up too high they'd shit alongside it on the floor. And now we were sleeping in it.

We had to stay in that shit-filled corridor each night for the weeks until Glen was released. Eventually, I was allowed back into Room 1 because I wasn't causing any trouble.

Glen's constant complaint was that he was broke, and if he only had some money he would be able to bribe his way out. When I had the chance to make a call again, I rang Anton at Four Horsemen and said, 'How much money have I got left?' The company still owed me salary which, if I hadn't been arrested, I guess they would have got around to paying me. I also knew there should be money coming into my account from some outside freelance jobs I had done. Anton said I had about US$20,000 still owing from Four Horsemen. I asked him to set aside some of that money for Glen. Anton said, 'We're already doing enough for you.' I replied that I knew a great deal about some of the company's activities, which I could easily share with authorities such as the FBI, and therefore it would be better to do as I asked. Anton quickly folded.

Over the next month, in meetings with the Australian embassy and Glen's lawyer, I arranged to pay US$17,000 so that justice officials could 'lose' the paperwork with Glen's original statement confessing to his crime. That eventually proved the key to getting him out. He wrote in his book that the money was paid by John Allen. John might have met him and said he would pay, but the actual money was mine, from the salary still owed to me by Four Horsemen. I also witnessed the paperwork Glen had to sign for his son's passport application. I did all these things for him because I felt genuinely sorry for his wife and three-year-old child, and also because I believed his promises that he would be able to help me from the outside.

It was quite an emotional scene when he left. We were sick

as dogs, thin and desperate. I pleaded with him, 'Don't let me rot in here, just help me when you get out.' Glen would write that we had made a suicide pact—that I promised to kill myself once I was without him. That was complete bullshit. Every day we would hit low patches where we talked about suicide, and I had managed to secrete a razor blade into my shoe to use in case of dire emergency. But there was no pact, just a cycle of moods we both went through before we kicked out of it again. I think Glen liked the idea that I had lost all hope and was going to commit suicide in jail, because it eased his conscience over what he did later.

Glen's last words to me on the day of his release were, 'I promise I'll sort things out for you and fix things up.'

He was called to leave, and disappeared across the yard through what I thought was the wrong door. Sure enough, a few moments later he came by again, shaking his head and grinning in embarrassment before heading the right way.

Glen came back to visit the jail quite regularly in the weeks after his release, at least once wearing a white coat, pretending to be a doctor, accompanied by Marcus Wilson. Glen said he was doing everything he could to get me out, including organising a bribe for the judge who had been assigned my case. I had to take him on trust. He kept saying with great confidence that he was 'sorting things out' for me, without progressing any further into details of his plans. I didn't know this, but he later claimed that he was 'working on a legal loophole' that enabled prisoners to spend one night outside with 'family' before their trial. For that night, a 'family member' took the prisoner's place in jail. What we would do, Glen planned, was pay an Afghan to be my 'family member'. During my night of freedom, I would skip the country, and then later we would pay a bribe to free the Afghan stand-in. Listening to Glen assuring me vaguely that he was 'getting shit organised' for me, I was having my doubts. I'm glad he didn't tell me at the time about his so-called 'legal loophole' plan, because I knew it was a complete prison myth, one of the many fantasies traded among inmates to while away the time and give them some hope, however false, while they waited to hear their fate. The 'loophole' was bullshit. Like a lot of stories in Afghanistan, it was just another way to separate people from their money.

My first court hearing, which rolled around soon after Glen's release, was in the fourth month after my arrest. Very little of the court process had been explained to me. Effectively, I had no lawyer. Leanne had given me a list of Afghan lawyers the embassy had checked out and reckoned were okay. The list didn't mean anything to me, so I picked the first name: Bashir. He came to see me once, but without an interpreter, and the meeting was useless. A short young guy with a square jaw and flowing hair, Bashir chattered away in Dari before giving me a reassuring smile and leaving.

A few days after Bashir's visit, the guards came into the cells and barked out a whole lot of words that of course I couldn't understand. They came over to me with a fresh set of folded prison pyjamas. The message was eventually conveyed that I had to get changed to go to court.

I was cuffed—hands together, with a vertical chain linking my wrists to my ankles. Police with AKs walked me for about ten minutes through various gates and buildings until we came to a busy building with painted mint-green interior walls. I was led into a medium-sized office full of overstuffed furniture surrounding a glass-topped table on which stood a vase of flowers and miniature Afghanistan flags. Already seated behind the desk were four middle-aged men in dark suits, who I took to be the judges. I was put in a heavy chair off to the side, and my chains were removed.

Flanked by two policemen, the judges were talking among themselves. I sat there wondering what was going on. There was no sign of Bashir or anyone from the embassy. Four Horsemen had sent an interpreter, for what it was worth. I had asked Anton if he could send Mohammed, a good man who had been my driver and interpreter throughout the previous six to eight months. Anton told me that Mohammed didn't work for Four Horsemen anymore. (Later, I found out that this was a lie and that Mohammed had wanted to come and help me, but the company had stopped him.) The actual interpreter they supplied for that first court hearing didn't like me, because he remembered a confrontation we had had in the office a few months earlier.

Since my earliest weeks at Four Horsemen, I'd worked out that, when we were out on the road getting shot at, the support from the office would be dependent on who was on duty in the Ops Room. Hiding behind my vehicle while someone was trying to kill me, I would phone Four Horsemen to send contact details, so the US military could react to it. But if it was time for dinner at the mess, forget about getting any support from the office. Usually I had to call up the Americans direct and ask them for a little top cover, simply because the expats at the office had gone out to eat and wouldn't answer the phone. Once, while under fire, I rang and rang and didn't get an answer. When I was able to make it back to the office after the contact was over, I stormed in to confront whomever was meant to be on duty.

There was an Afghan sitting there watching porn on the internet. The possibility that I might have died because this fucker was too busy having a wank to answer the phone was too much. He understood what the extent of the Ops Room duties were after our discussion. I did, however, have to get a new keyboard for the Ops Room.

If you can't do the job, go fuck yourself. But on your own time.

Anyway, what goes around comes around, I guess: the Afghan guy I'd gone off at that night was now the interpreter Four Horsemen had sent to my court hearing. I never found out if it was a coincidence, or a cruel joke at my expense. In the court room, I tried to be nice to him but it didn't do me any good. He ignored me. He probably hated my guts.

So I was on my own. My lawyer hadn't turned up, the embassy didn't seem to know my hearing was happening, and Four Horsemen had sent the least helpful person on their entire staff. Great. The other person in the room was a youngish, redheaded westerner. His name was Jeremy Kelly. Unfortunately, I knew who he was.

Kelly had come to Afghanistan on the coattails of an Australian cameraman. Both of them fancied themselves as war correspondents, and the cameraman got into trouble and disappeared. More or less as soon as he arrived in the country, Kelly had been locked up in Tolkeef. This was before my arrest, and he was let go after a short time.

In my first month in jail, Jeremy Kelly had turned up looking for 'Rob', which was also the name of the cameraman he couldn't find. The guards brought out Glen and me. Kelly sniffed a scoop and asked if he could interview us. He said he worked for *The Australian*, but actually he was a freelancer or stringer, hoping to find stuff and sell it to whoever he could talk into buying. I said to him, 'I'll talk to you, but before you do anything with it you've got to wait until we get out of here, because if you publish while we're still in here you can fuck it up for all of us.'

'Sure, sure,' he said, eager to agree to anything.

Of course, between then and the court hearing, he violated our agreement and broke the story of my arrest. I had still been clinging to the hope that some quiet bribes could get me out, but his story had torpedoed that plan. As soon as there was media attention, I would be treated as a high-profile prisoner the Afghans couldn't release quietly. The first consideration, for them, was whether any action would gain or lose them face. If I was a nobody, it mightn't have mattered either way if they let me go. But now that I was in the international media, to release me would hold them up to ridicule. Whatever chance I had had, Kelly had blown it for me. When I arrived at that first court hearing, I said, 'I'm not talking to you.'

I couldn't believe he was even allowed into the court. The embassy had explained to me that, under Afghan law, you could ask for no media coverage of your trial. I said to the judge, 'I don't want him in here. He's a journalist and I don't want any media coverage.'

The judge, whose name was Baktiari, said, 'No, he's from the embassy.'

Kelly just sat there with a smug look on his face.

Judge Baktiari began reading in Dari. Bizarrely, he didn't have any shoes on. He was trussed up behind his vase of flowers and Afghanistan flags, but all I could look at were his big toenails poking out from under his desk.

Baktiari spoke for about five minutes. I was asking the company interpreter what he was saying.

'Sh! Sh! I'm listening!' the terp hissed.

Part of the way through the judge's spiel, Bashir turned up in a double-breasted grey suit. He took no part in the proceedings.

Once the judge was finished, I was given no hint of what he was saying. Maybe the terp didn't want to be the bearer of bad news. The cops cuffed me again and marched me out. I said to Bashir and the terp, 'What the fuck just happened?' Jeremy Kelly, who was listening to a translation and taking notes, said nothing to me; Bashir likewise. The company interpreter: silence.

As I was exiting, Glen turned up in the corridor, looking flustered and disorganised, and too late. I couldn't tell him what had happened, because I didn't know.

I was walked to Tolkeef, back through all the gates and hallways, asking my guards what had gone on. They said nothing. I thought it must have been a preliminary hearing, and maybe the judge had set out a statement of police facts and proposed a date for the proper trial. So I wasn't feeling so bad until we got back to the jail. One of the guards spoke a little English.

'Big problem,' he said, shaking his head.

'What's the problem?'

He ran a finger across his throat. 'You have been given the death sentence.'

What the fuck? *That* was it? Aside from the ridiculous nature of the hearing—five to ten minutes, a speech from a judge with no shoes, no effective interpreter or lawyer, nobody from the embassy, only Jeremy Kelly—what about the evidence? Was I going to hang based on the Four Horsemen-prepared statement that Anton had got me to sign the day after my arrest? Or based on the questions the counter-terrorism guy had asked me? How could that be? That was still the only time I had been formally questioned. And what about other witnesses? If anyone had made a statement against me, why wasn't he in court?

I called Katie, in shock. She just said very firmly and flatly, 'It's not going to happen.' She calmed me down a little. It was surreal. She was sitting on her back veranda at Port Augusta, amid preparations for our mother's 60th birthday party, and was reassuring her brother in Afghanistan that he was not going to be executed. Maybe even more surreal, at the party itself, people who didn't know where I was asked Katie why I hadn't made it. 'Oh, he just couldn't get away,' she said with typical black humour. But at her core, Katie is an optimist and a problem solver, and she reacted to the death sentence as just another obstacle we had to find our way past.

To me, though, it was the first time the death penalty had been on the table and I was stressing out. Completely at sea, I rang the person in Kabul I felt I could rely on most. In my naïvety, that happened to be Glen. He came and saw me that afternoon, in a sombre mood.

'You'd have been released earlier except that the Australian media campaigned too soon,' he said.

'The only media that has mentioned me is Jeremy Kelly.'

Glen asked how else he could help me. I said, 'You've got to tell the embassy, and make sure they can monitor me here and stop me from being sent to Pol-e-Charkhi.'

'Sure, I'll set that in motion,' Glen said. He was certain there had to be someone else we could pay to get me out, just as I'd done to get him out. He said the judge had been open to a payment to reduce the charge against me, but that had been scuppered by Jeremy Kelly's story. All the same, Glen still acted as if he was hopeful. He went on, 'I'll look after all your stuff. Just sign it over to me so I can pick up the rest of your money.' The embassy had about US$5000 of mine that they managed to get back somehow from the Afghan authorities after my arrest. I signed it over to Glen.

And that was it. Gone. All of it went. He also took my vintage leather jacket that had been found at my apartment at Four Horsemen. For some reason, I found that particularly low. Why would you do that to anybody, let alone someone who has helped you escape—to whom you 'owe your life'? It's pretty demoralising when someone smashes everything you share. Once he had my money, it seems his commitment to my freedom faded away.

It was years before I got to the bottom of what Glen had really done. I thought he was just a con man. But after I had been in prison for about five years, I asked Hakemi, a Taliban mufti, or legal expert, with whom I built up a rapport, if he could get my file from the prison authorities. Hakemi had ways of obtaining information. He asked for 'the Australian's file', but when he brought it into my cell, he couldn't understand it.

Reading it, he shook his head. 'This has got nothing about murder. This says you've been lying with a child.'

'What?' I said.

'That's what it says,' Hakemi went on. 'Oh, hold on, it's not you. Who is this man?

'What's his name?' I said.

Hakemi read out the name that Glen had taken on when he converted to Islam. As he read through the file, Hakemi said, 'Do you know where this man lives?'

'Not any more,' I said. 'He's probably in Australia or the UK.'

It seems that Glen had been caught out by Zara with one of the the many street kids around Kabul. When she went to the Afghan Police and filed a written complaint, all they saw were dollar signs: a westerner illegally married to an Afghan woman equals a big payday. Whether it was true or not is irrelevant—illegal marriage is a far bigger deal than child prostitution in that country.

Glen hung around in Afghanistan for a while after his release. When Belinda eventually got over to visit me in jail, after one look at him she said to me, 'Don't trust this guy, there's something not right about him.' I learnt my lesson, but too late. When I first met Glen, it was more important to trust *someone* than to judge whether they were worth trusting.

Ivan had let me know that Belinda was in the country and was coming to the jail. I went to the 'visitors' area'; as usual, it was bedlam, with dozens of people on both sides screaming their messages at each other, trying to make themselves heard. Belinda and I worked our way to the fence on each side. It was fantastic to see her, but far from ideal—amid the crush, we only had a couple of holes in the chainlink to speak and see through. She was only able to stay for less than ten minutes, and we couldn't say much as we were being shoved and punched and shouted over. The cops were making things worse, patrolling to smack people's hands if they were trying to pass money, food or phones through the fence, and this caused a domino effect of people falling against each other. The noise was overwhelming.

Aside from seeing each other, which was precious, there was no meaningful communication between Belinda and me that day. But the next day, the embassy staff brought her with them, and I was able to sit down with her in the office where

I also met the Australians from the embassy. This time it went a bit better: it was emotional, and Belinda wanted to know what was going to happen to me, but I had as little idea as she had. We had about three-quarters of an hour together, often interrupted by Afghan officers walking in to tell me to boast to her how well they were treating me. So I had to brush them off.

Belinda has a good heart and hated seeing the surrounding chaos and the state I was in. Seeing the strain and confusion on her face, which she was trying very hard to hide, I was tortured by guilt. Did she really need to be dragged into this? We had been together for nearly six months in South Africa before I took the job in Afghanistan. I was then away for six months, and saw her again in January for a month when I went back to Cape Town on leave. By now, we were placing enormous weight on what was still a relatively new relationship. After the meeting, I was a wreck. While we were talking, I'd been hiding as much as she had. I didn't want to show any weakness—this was my constant condition now, acting tough—and this put a further limit on how much we could show each other. She was hopeful, saying things like, 'You'll get out soon, you'll be all right', and I was doing my tough-guy thing, grunting that she shouldn't expect me out any time soon. She was making plans for us both, and I would pull her up, saying, 'Let's just see how this plays out first. I'm not quite sure how it's going to go.'

They let me ring her that night, and she was able to come to the prison on her own a couple more times during the week that she was there. She was cluey, wearing a scarf and dressing down, and catching taxis on her own, and it kept me alive to see her, though I didn't let this show.

What I also couldn't show was fear. I had been condemned to death. I couldn't even get my head around this. How could I lose my life on the basis of a five-minute court hearing in which I wasn't allowed to speak? I didn't understand. I couldn't visualise what an actual execution would be like. There had to be more checks and balances. I had to get a chance to defend myself. It wasn't until later, when I was moved to Pol-e-Charkhi, that the reality of a death sentence sank in. While I was at Tolkeef, which was only a remand prison, inmates would go around telling people that they had received the death penalty as a way of making themselves seem untouchable, not to be messed with, like they had nothing to lose. It was a bluff. Only after I got to Pol-e-Charkhi did I see what death looked like. When I was first sentenced, it was so preposterous I could still keep it at arm's length.

What hit me harder was the news that one of my closest mates at Four Horsemen had been killed.

5

Enemies within

When I first went to Afghanistan in 2008, after more than fourteen years in the Australian Army and nearly four more working in private security in Iraq, I was burnt out in some deep and fundamental way that I couldn't put into words. What I couldn't say, my actions said for me. At the end of my stint in Iraq in 2007 I went back to Cape Town, where the mutually destructive relationship I was in ended rather spectacularly. I tried pretty much anything illicit, dangerous or stupid to try to fill the hole. I was a mess. Eventually a friend said to me, 'If you want to kill yourself, do it in Afghanistan or Iraq. We don't want to see you do it here.' *Fuck it*, I thought, *that's a plan—back on the tools*. I was running out of money anyway and it was easier to get work overseas than in South Africa.

I asked around, intentionally seeking out the most dangerous work. A close mate in Cape Town, an ex-sniper from the UK, said, 'If you want silly shit, hook up with John Allen, his company are doing that sort of thing.' I sent my CV to Four Horsemen, and a few months later they hired me to go to Afghanistan.

The cruel irony was that I met Belinda in the months between receiving the offer from Four Horsemen and leaving South Africa. I would have seven years to contemplate what might have been.

When I stepped out of the plane into Kabul International in the summer of 2008, the airport was chaotic, visitors having shouting matches with customs officers who were trying to rip them off or tell them their visas weren't correct. As in Iraq, there were a lot of new computers and security equipment not plugged in and not being used. Someone's idea of reconstruction was to fly in a lot of expensive gear and leave it there until the locals figured out how to use it.

Outside, Kabul was a lot wilder than Baghdad. The security situation was free enough that you could catch a taxi, which you would not do in Baghdad while I was there, and which you could soon not do in Kabul, either. In 2008, Kabul was what I'd imagine a city like Abu Dhabi had been like twenty-five to thirty years earlier: dusty and undeveloped, with potholed roads and a clusterfuck of patched-up cars, livestock-drawn carts and every now and then a convoy of black Lexus SUVs screaming through, smashing everyone out of the way, so that some Afghan VIP could get to lunch.

The driver from Four Horsemen took me through the oddly specialised shopping districts. There was chicken street, that sold only chickens; meat street; pots and pans street; electronics street; rugs street. No wonder they don't make any money. How is the retailer ever going to win when the consumer can just bob from shop to shop playing them off against each other until he gets the deal he wants?

As I passed through the city for the first time, I wasn't nervous. I feel at home in places like that and when I'm by myself. I have a tendency to step back and observe what's going on, which is easier when no one knows you and you're in a different culture. You deal with people respectfully and don't try to bend them to your ways. You cut your own path and get on with the job at hand. I was soon to learn the limits and consequences of that philosophy.

If I arrived with a jaded view of my life and the world, the person who did most to change that and set me on a better course was John Allen.

I met John when I got to Kabul. He was in his late forties, short and stocky, with crewcut dark hair and a moustache. A very gregarious, friendly guy, he came originally from New Jersey but now lived in New Mexico when he wasn't supervising company activities from the US or here in Kabul. He walked with a limp and sometimes wore an eye patch; when he didn't wear it, that eye was a bit flat-looking. It was still his own eye, but was blind, filled with oil.

The limp and the sightless eye were reminders of his wild past. I'd heard legends about John over the years. He had a reputation for being a cowboy. He had made his name with the US 7th Special Forces group, as an 18B, the US Army's designation for an SF Weapons Specialist. He could still shoot better than most, even with one eye. On his third trip to Afghanistan with Special Forces, John had got fucked up badly in a firefight. He should have been killed, but got away intact except for one eye and part of his right knee. He was retired after that, but two weeks after getting out of hospital, he was back in Afghanistan setting up his company, which he named, dramatically, after the Four Horsemen of the Apocalypse. There were many stories kicking around of John's time in Afghanistan, not only with the army but with other government agencies and as a contractor.

The main role of the US Special Forces is in unconventional warfare, taking insurgents on at their own game and training locals in basic tactics, organisation and small arms use, leading and advising where necessary. They also provide military and civilian aid, and medical care to friendly locals—all this 'hearts and minds' is a far better way of getting people onside and fighting the bad guys with the bonus (for politicians) of fewer US casualties.

I was shown around the compound, which housed about thirty or forty people: mainly Afghans, also Americans, Macedonians and Kenyans, and now me.

The Four Horsemen compound was typical for Kabul, a shit-tin of poorly constructed buildings crammed into a standard-sized city block enclosed behind a fortified front gate manned by Afghan guards. John had built a small mosque in the middle of the compound, even though there was a public mosque down the road. He had a keen sense of what was valued in this society, and wanted to make it known that he was a friend of the Afghans.

To live in, the staff had a couple of houses fronting the street, which I wasn't too comfortable about. We also had a building in which to work on our vehicles, mostly Toyota Surfs and LandCruisers.

Even with the fortified gate and the guardhouse, the lack of security at the compound bothered me. As would often be the case in Kabul, there was always building work going on, which meant there were too many eyes around the place for comfort. My default position was to distrust the Afghans, including those who worked for us, and the labourers blowing in and out each day set me on edge.

I lived in a tiny room in an apartment on the second floor along with five other expats. Over the time I was there, we fortified the apartment inside by sandbagging walls and installing screens inside the windows so that no interior movement could be seen. We also stocked the apartment with ammunition. John's room had its own running water and was basically an armoury; he had every weapon that opened and shut in there.

The room I moved into was a converted bathroom. They had pulled all the fixtures out and laid plywood on the floor because they didn't have enough bedrooms. (Yes, there was another bathroom.) I didn't mind it because it had thick walls, no windows and only one door. A bomb could go off outside those walls and not hurt me. There was a water tap, so if push came to shove I could barricade myself in for a long time. I had no mattress. I slept on the floor, which I'd always liked. Even in the army I used to sleep on the floor. People would come into the converted bathroom and look around and say, 'Where's your bed?' Nah, not for me.

For food, we had to look after ourselves. When Four Horsemen had emailed me to offer the job, they said my food would be included, but the reality was that company employees had to go outside and source it themselves. We could go to the mess of any American military facility, but travelling around Kabul and entering a place that was a target for the insurgency posed extra risks. I tried to convince Petar not to expose us when our whole purpose of being there was to negate risk, but my suggestions fell on deaf ears. So we had to go out and either buy food, go to a restaurant to eat, or find a safe way to get into an American base.

While I had a lot of respect for John Allen, he was often not in the country and from day one I could see that corruption and dodges ran through the company at every level. Half the people working for Four Horsemen were working for multiple outside employers or themselves, or had some secret business going on.

The first dodge I noticed was with our weapons. When I'd been in Iraq, the licensing of weapons was strictly run by the Iraqi government. If anything, it was over-bureaucratic. We used to complain about needing weapons cards and proper registration for every last thing, but it did mean that they couldn't rip us off and take our weapons or cars away. In Afghanistan, on the other hand, you lost your car or your weapons on a regular basis because you'd pissed some war lord off. He would tell one of his mates that your licence had run out, and they would come and confiscate your stuff until they could verify your licence, which they couldn't because there was no real system to control the the licences to start with. If you didn't pay a bribe to keep your gun, you couldn't do your business. Contractors found themselves out of work for a month purely because they'd refused to pay someone a backhander. Even the military were saying, 'Just pay it.' That pissed me off. Once you submitted to it, they would do it again, especially Afghans, who've been doing it ever since westerners have been in the country.

I quickly learnt why Afghans were such great survivors; that's what I admire about them. Their country has been taken over by the British, the Russians and now an American-led western Coalition, but they're still there, still running things their way. A key part of this survival instinct is the unimportance of words. Over the years, they learnt to say anything, if it meant getting through the day. Are you a

Muslim or a heathen? I'm a Muslim, just don't cut my head off. Are you a communist or a mujahideen? I'm a communist, just don't cut my head off. They say what's necessary to get by. It's in their culture to say what they think you want to hear, including good news, so you don't get pissed off. They just want things to float. Like I say, I do admire that, but it made Kabul a fucking difficult place to work because, basically, you couldn't trust anybody to tell the truth.

At the centre of this web, in our little world, was Commander Haussedin.

His protection and status came from the fact that he was married to a sister of Ahmad Shah Massoud, the former leader of the Northern Alliance. Known as the 'Lion of Panjshir', Massoud led the Northern Alliance against the Russians from 1979 to 1989, held power until the Taliban revolution in 1996, and was assassinated, probably by Al-Qaeda, two days before the attacks on America in September 2001. In much of Afghanistan, Massoud was revered as a martyr, and anyone connected with him was able to use his name to attain influence.

Commander Haussedin, from Massoud's Panjshiri clan, ran Massoud's prison for him back in the 1990s. When I was there Haussedin still had his own private prison. The NDS, the Afghan secret service, were mostly Panjshiris and they used Haussedin's prison, but he was skilled at playing both sides of the fence. The Panjshiris would go on about how they saved Afghanistan from the Russians and then from the Taliban, but they were the ones who cut a deal with the Russians not to get attacked, they were the ones who sent weapons to the Taliban to swap for opium so they could ship it out and keep their cash flow, and they were the ones who then fought alongside the Taliban against Coalition forces.

Commander Haussedin rode in a Lexus but he also had three LandCruisers, black tinted-window mafia-style vehicles, and fifteen to thirty guards he kept with him when he moved about. He controlled security at the main American camp inside Kabul and had a free pass to come and go as he liked: the photo of Shah Massoud in his window was good enough. Everyone knew who he was.

Haussedin had fingers in lots of pies. The big American base at Kabul was surrounded by a buffer zone, in which a market was set up and some of the personnel could go to buy stuff on their days off. Haussedin controlled the security on the perimeter of that zone. No Afghans could work there unless they gave him a cut, and he controlled much of the local access to the American base. A lot of people who could have helped the Americans improve the country were blocked, simply because they wouldn't pay Haussedin his kickback.

He loved to look the part, cruising around in a big black coat with military boots he claimed to have taken off the Russians during the war. He also wore American medals with matching ribbons. What the fuck was that about— were the Americans that corrupt or stupid that they would give this prick a medal? I later found out that when he was inside the American base in Kabul once, Haussedin saw two Russians walking around. He told the Americans that they were spies. The Americans arrested them, and gave him a medal. But the thing was, Haussedin knew those guys were Russian secret service agents because he'd been *in business* with them. KGB men, after the collapse of the Iron Curtain, often moved into mafia work in Afghanistan, sorting out shipments of drugs to Russia. They were in negotiations for a new deal, and Haussedin found out that they were talking to his competitors to get a better price. So he did the Afghan thing: he invited them to the US base to show them around. He let them walk in, and then told the Americans that they were spies. That's how he dealt with things. Always working an angle, especially when he was smiling.

The people around him weren't all bad. His driver spoke English and was a decent guy, and his younger son was all right. But Haussedin got his jollies from kicking the son until he pissed himself in front of a group of laughing bodyguards. The Afghans in the compound were terrified of him.

Why did a security company run by John Allen have anything to do with these types? As always, the reasons went deep into the past. When the Russians had run Afghanistan, their military controlled all the building and reconstruction work in the country and shut out the locals. When the Americans moved in, someone in their infinite wisdom decided that nation-building would be better served by giving jobs to the impoverished Afghan people. So instead of using their own military to truck materials through the country, the Americans invited private local companies to tender.

The local company that won the tender would send its trucks to the border with Pakistan to pick up the shipments. Afghanistan is landlocked, but some companies had access to the sea ports in Pakistan to pick up connexes (shipping containers) with Humvees in them, and even weapons coming in by boat to Pakistan. Essentially the Afghan trucking company got the tender, the driver got a piece of paper with the manifest number on it, and off he went to a cooling-off area where the shipment had to wait twenty-four hours so someone could make sure it wasn't about to blow up. Then the Afghan trucking company delivered it to the Americans, handing over the piece of paper, and went off to its next job.

The big problem with that arrangement was security. Without military protection, these truck convoys would get blown up by roadside bombs, shot at by insurgents, or raided in the open country. As the transport function had been privatised, so now was the security. The trucking company partnered up with a security company. Some expats, such as John Allen, saw the opportunity in this wave of privatisation, but they couldn't run as foreign companies; they had to have an Afghan element in the hierarchy, as well as Afghan staff security. Hence the need for a war lord such as Commander Haussedin, who had enough manpower at his command and the clout to organise them.

The problem was, the people who could arrange the muscle were also the country's biggest thugs and pirates. If they had this piece of paper—the trucking and security contract—they couldn't be touched by any authority, as the contract gave them the status of a military convoy. But they had no loyalty. If they didn't have a job on the next day, they would hire themselves out to the Taliban. They were as likely to shoot us as help us.

Haussedin's smuggling of arms and drugs was rampant. The UN would write off captured weapons and send them to its decommissioning plant in Jalalabad. As I said before, Haussedin had a relative in the plant, who would hand over the undestroyed weapons to him. He took them to Taliban areas and swapped them for opium, which he would send out of the country after trucking it around on our convoys! When he had to work with some idiot Australian ex-grunt with borderline OCD like me, who kept track of paperwork for every last thing, he quickly found that I was cramping his style.

On one of my first trips on my own, I was counting the trucks and came up with a few extra.

'Hey, you've got a couple of extra trucks. What's in this truck?'

Haussedin's security team leader, Anar Gul, said, 'That's for the US Army.'

I looked in the truck. It was full of logs, bundled up and tied with hemp rope.

'Yes! Firewood for the US Army!' he cried.

'I'm pretty sure the Yanks don't need firewood, champ.'

I looked under the firewood and there were packages of what looked like drugs: plastic shopping bags wrapped heavily in brown masking tape. A convoy was a great place to stash opium, because it could move around the country under armed guard, paid for by the US Army.

'Sorry fellas, you're on your own,' I said.

Scowling, Anar Gal told the extra drivers to go but after a few kilometres they were right up the arse of the convoy again—where I usually travelled. I halted the convoy again, walked down to the extra trucks and shot out the front tyres of every one.

That type of behaviour put a lot of people's noses out of joint.

As I settled into life in Kabul, I got a release from the corrupt and weird relationships within Four Horsemen by catching up with colleagues from my old unit, the 1st Battalion 1RAR, or simply the 'Bn' by its members, who were now working privately in the PSC (private security company) sector. Officially, there was not meant to be any fraternisation between contractors such as myself and serving military, who were not meant to leave their base for non-operational reasons. But some of those still in would come out to meet us at an old English pub called the Gandamak, run by a British ex-military guy, which was safe and secure. Another place called La Cantina, a Mexican restaurant in Kabul run by two Aussie girls from Queensland, had a big Australian and Kiwi clientele. Another restaurant called Sizzler sold almost the entire Penfolds range over the bar. We had an epic 1RAR reunion there that resulted in us all being removed by the Afghan street guards at gunpoint. Some people have no sense of humour.

Many of my old colleagues were in Afghanistan doing the same sort of thing as me, using our skills in the private sector. We were also able to catch up with guys who had gone over to SF who, because of who they are and how they behave, were allowed out. They were adults and remained low profile. It was when you got a young wannabe football hero, who hated Muslims because he'd never been out of his state until he joined the National Guard, and who hadn't had a drink in a while, that you got trouble. By contrast, the guys working in SF teams were working hard outside the wire, not shuffling papers and complaining that war is hell, and they could be trusted to let their hair down sensibly. Well, mostly anyway.

I might have been trying to convince myself I didn't give a shit about anything when I arrived in Afghanistan, but within weeks of arriving, once I understood how the whole system ran and how everyone was at the mercy of Haussedin and war lords like him, I was more pissed off than reckless. I didn't want to get killed by these guys. I didn't want to get killed at all.

It was hard to figure out why John Allen would tolerate them. But more and more I began to see how John had his blind spots, so to speak. The biggest of these blind spots, even bigger than the Haussedin and the Macedonians, was John's number two, Kyle. Four Horsemen's head of business development liked to be called 'Sir'. He'd previously been a lieutenant colonel in the US Army. He had started in the US military in artillery, but was moved to ordnance, which spoke volumes to anyone who knows army language and politics. No one who has joined an army to fight willingly leaves an arms corps. If you have been moved from an arms corps to an administrative or logistics corps—for example, from artillery to ordnance—it generally says you're broken, and you've been sacked or kicked sideways.

Kyle liked his gear and went out of his way to get what he could from his contacts in the military. Anything bright and shiny was hanging off him. 'What do you need all that shit for when you're only going out to the embassy, Kyle?' I would ask.

Coming from a kit monster as bad as myself, that's saying something. But some of the gear Kyle got could have been put to better use on ops on the road instead of for photo ops at the US embassy.

This wasn't the only reason I refused to call him 'Sir'.

The main reason I couldn't respect Kyle was that he was dodgy. I pulled him (and John) up about Haussedin on more than one occasion, but they weren't interested. Kyle was playing a bigger game. His main role with the company was 'contract development', which meant wining and dining US military types. In a big military operation, there is always sneaky stuff going on. I wasn't above bringing in a couple of cartons of beer or a bottle of whiskey to Special Forces guys. One of the benefits of going in and out of South Africa, where I went when I had any decent time off, was that the country had no embargoes against Cuba, so I could buy and bring back much-appreciated Cuban cigars for friends in the American military. Kyle, on the other hand, brought in contraband on an industrial scale, anything he thought might help him keep or win a contract, and all the better if it was exploiting a weakness that someone would prefer nobody to know about. He took his military buddies drinking and whoring, even though they tended to be married. I am not morally judgemental about this. I'd done a job in Cape Town with clients mixed up in that particular business. It's part and parcel of being in the security industry, or any industry for that matter, that you have clients you don't like. But this was in a different league. Serving US officers who experienced Kyle's hospitality would ask him which trucking companies to give contracts, and the companies would then pay money to Haussedin and we would get the security side. It was everything the most cynical person would suspect was going on in Afghanistan, only worse.

Some of what Kyle did was harmless and ridiculous. We wrote reports of all of our activities out on the road, and he would put his own little spin on them, sometimes inserting his name into the top of the report, and take them to the US embassy to pass onto the various agencies he spoke to there. He never read them through though, and when I figured out what he was doing, I would insert random phrases into the reports—something like the words, 'You're a fuckwit' in the middle of a detail on where a convoy moved. Because he never said anything to me about that, I could tell that he never read them. I hoped that someone did, somewhere, and had a laugh at Kyle's expense.

His habits really rubbed me up the wrong way when it compromised our safety out on the road. We would get the contracts, but not the safety equipment and arms that were expressly part of those contracts. For one contract I worked on, Kyle budgeted for ten expat security staff, thirty Afghans, and weapons including M4s, M249s and M240s. The military accepted that and paid us for those requirements: a US$5 million contract. The job was to move Mine Resistant Armoured Personnel Carrier (MRAPs) vehicles from Forward Operating Bases (FOBs) around the country to and from Bagram, swapping out new ones for old. It required a lot of daylight movement of military material and military trucks. Everybody shoots at you, and it's bloody dangerous. But instead of the thirty staff and a shit-tin of weapons, the security was actually carried out by me and a team of twenty to twenty-five Afghans. We were running out of ammunition all the time, we were in that many fights, and I was having to buy more ammo out of my own pocket. I even had to call my sister Katie to ask her to lend me money to buy ammunition. She couldn't believe it, and that conversation sowed the first seed of doubt in her mind about Four Horsemen.

For Kyle, it was all about the bottom dollar. He was on profit share, and manipulated the supply of material if he could bump up his monthly numbers. I knew when the military paid us, but he would sit on the money until the end of the month, inflating the company bank account. When he came into my room to give me a Warning Order for an upcoming job one afternoon, I said, 'I'm not doing it until I get paid, Kyle. This is not the military. Pay me, then I'll do it.'

Kyle looked a bit taken aback. 'Are you serious?'

'Fucking oath, mate. Union rules.'

'Well, if you won't go out you're fucking fired then!' he said, and stormed off.

'Okay, awesome.'

Fifteen minutes later, presumably after a flurry of emails, John Allen rang up and said, 'You're not fired. Have you been paid yet? No? I'll pay you out of my own bank account.'

Unfortunately this would happen to all the staff and most didn't have the access to the boss to sort it out.

I couldn't work out why John was loyal to Kyle. They got on well together, and I suppose they had their own secrets and invisible bonds of loyalty. But it grated on me, because I had such a genuine and maybe naïve respect for John.

'Kyle's a prick, you realise that, don't you?' I said.

'Oh, he's doing his best,' John would reply.

On top of the dangerous crap involving Haussedin and the incompetence of the Macedonians, I was keen to get away from all of this. For six grand a month, which was what I was getting at the start, I wasn't going to get shot up due to some lazy idiot in the office. Getting smacked for your own fuck-ups is bad enough.

Aside from John Allen, the only fellow employee at Four Horsemen that I trusted was a younger American, Junior.

Junior was ex-military police, a smart-arse from Texas. He and I hit it off straight away. In Iraq, his unit had been the one that was notoriously ambushed in Sadr City in Baghdad in April 2004 when the Americans had gone in to break up the 'Mahdi Army' insurgency bloc of the cleric Muqtada-al-Sadr. They had been hunted back out again, shot to shit on that day, leading to a siege that ended up lasting for months. Eight American troops were killed, including their unit Commanding Officer and Top Sergeant, and more than fifty were wounded on the first day alone.

Junior had been one of the wounded that day. He received a Purple Heart and left the army soon after, transferring to the reserves as many US veterans did. He spent a bit of time away from the Middle East, but then joined Four Horsemen. Junior started out running a team on the road like I did, then moved into the office, getting involved in the operations and business development side of things.

He was a good kid: he could work stuff out and talk his way out of anything. Without the same verbal skills and front, I came to rely on him in tricky situations. One night in Kabul, Junior said, 'I need you to pick up some ammunition for one of the other crews and bring it to the house.' He didn't tell me exactly what I was picking up, and I was somewhat disturbed: I ended up with 50,000 rounds of PKM ammunition, 40 RPG rockets and about twenty big steel tins of AK rounds. It was enough for a major battle. Because Kyle wasn't getting us the gear that our contract required, and because then President Hamid Karzai wanted to stop American arms and ammunition coming into the country, we were working to supply ourselves from the black market. Unsatisfactory for us, but very nice for arms traffickers such as Commander Haussedin.

Inevitably, while I was driving all this ammo back to the compound, I got pulled up at a police checkpoint. I thought, *This is not cool*. One of the cops came over to the car just as I locked all the doors and Mohammed, my driver, began verbally tap-dancing.

'He wants us to get out of the car,' he said.

'Yeah, like that's going to fucking happen,' I said, madly speed-dialling Junior's number.

'He wants us to get out,' he repeated, while the cop was banging on the window and yelling.

My call got though. 'Junior! Get the fuck down here!'

Junior left the office straight away. In the meantime, the police surrounded the car. We were licensed for various things, but not to be carrying around this quantity of ammunition. In any case, the licensing system was so nebulous that the police were more likely to do what they felt like in the moment, which could easily be to confiscate the ammunition and throw me in a cell.

While this was being decided, Junior arrived.

'Hey man, it's all cool,' he announced to the police, pressing the flesh, giving away little torches and packets of cigarettes—real American ones, not Chinese knock-offs.

I thought, *This is going to go one way or the other.*

Fortunately, it went Junior's way, as things usually did. He convinced them that there was no problem with us having all this ammo, and furthermore, when they finished in the police force, these guys would have jobs with us! All good, no worries. And I managed to not get arrested. That could have been nasty. They were a bit funny about high-explosive shit inside Kabul.

Junior and I would go out drinking and look around the town together. *Whiskey Tango Foxtrot*, the Tina Fey movie with a lot of scenes of wild after-dark partying among expats in Kabul, is actually a toned-down version of what was going on. It was a party town back then, and although I didn't have a lot of big nights out, it was guaranteed when I was with Junior.

He told me a lot of stories about his time in Iraq. Part of his unit was mixed up in the scandal at the Abu Ghraib jail in Baghdad, when videos had come out of junior soldiers abusing prisoners. According to Junior, the ones who got caught were a bunch of young guys and girls who saw the spooks doing this kind of shit, and decided to do it themselves while the spooks weren't around, and took photos. As young people do. Junior said that the people in charge of the unit, not to mention some of the spooks themselves, should have got into trouble as well. In the US military, he said, officers and NCOs tended not to take responsibility for the actions of those below them if they could get away with it. 'The kids got their arses kicked,' he said, 'but the officers knew it was going on and should have got theirs kicked as well.'

Junior was the first person who warned me never to turn my back on Commander Haussedin. When I was first at the company, Junior said about Haussedin and his cronies: 'They're pieces of shit, but we have to work with them because they control everything and that's the way it's done.'

Because of Haussedin's power, we still had to clean up the mess he created. Junior and I went sometimes to a restaurant near Bagram, beside the buffer area that Haussedin controlled. Once, while we were at our compound, we got a phone call from Haussedin's son and driver, who was a decent guy. He said, 'The commander is sick and is shooting up this restaurant because they're trying to get him to pay the bill.'

We knew what 'sick' meant: Haussedin had been smoking opium again. After the meal, when the restaurant people had asked him to pay his bill, he had exploded: 'I'm Commander Haussedin, I knew Shah Massoud!' He threatened to kill the restaurateur and pulled out his pistol.

When Junior and I turned up with one of the Nepalese from the company, Haussedin had long gone but the place was in a mess. Junior went inside and smoothed things over while I stood overwatch in the dark outside. That's how we worked: he sweet-talked everyone and I was the head-kicker. Diplomat and thug. If people wanted to argue with Junior, I would step out of the dark with the ink on my arms, all tooled up. It freaked people out and they soon came around to a compromise. But this time, due to Junior's diplomatic skills, we were soon all drinking tea together.

I loved the guy. About a month after I was arrested, while I was still in Tolkeef, I managed to get him on the phone. By then he couldn't really do anything for me. The company had cut me loose and Junior was still working for them, and I understood that he was limited by that. Four Horsemen didn't want him or anyone else talking to me.

'Dude, I'm leaving the company,' he said.

'What? Why?'

'Because of the obvious.'

I left that hanging. We were conscious that someone might be listening in on our calls, so he didn't elaborate. He told me he was going to work with another company. I wished him well, and told him to try to stay in contact as far as possible. Two days later, he died.

At the time, you could drive from the Four Horsemen compound to Bagram pretty safely. The Taliban didn't fuck around near Bagram because it was too dangerous for them. They had learnt from their war with the Russians that if they attacked too close to the airports, they were walking into the most fortified areas. They still fired mortar rounds at Bagram on rare occasions, but were smart enough to not get too close. There was a lot of Kabuli commercial activity out there, and if the Taliban attacked, they could turn all the locals against them.

Two days after our last phone conversation, Junior was in a car with two Lebanese guys from the company he was about to join. On their way to Bagram, on that supposedly safe road, they were blown up by a roadside bomb and killed instantly.

My sadness, when I got the news, was soon overcome

by suspicion. It didn't sit well with me that he'd said he was leaving the company because of 'the obvious', a month and a half after my arrest, and then he died two days later in a bomb attack that was unlikely to have been Taliban, in an area, on the fringes of Bagram, controlled by Haussedin's militia. And that he was with employees of the company he was moving to, who also died. Since my arrest, I was starting to see Four Horsemen in a completely different light—or maybe all the dirt that I'd tried to ignore was coming to the surface.

Within a short time of Junior's death, two officers from the FBI came to question me in prison. They were stern-looking men wearing checked shirts and 511 brand trousers, the uniform that they all wore to look low-profile but which was so universal that everyone could identify them on sight.

They asked me if there was any reason Junior might have been killed by anyone other than the Taliban or the insurgency.

I didn't know whether I could trust them. 'Probably,' I said, 'but I can't tell you while I'm here. It's too dangerous for me.'

They said that they understood. I wished I could have said more. Junior had been my closest friend at Four Horsemen, and the one who had warned me about Haussedin. In the last few weeks, after I had been stitched up, Junior must have decided it was too risky to stay with the company and work like that. He had set up some of the upcoming contracts with Kyle, and was now going to walk away to a new company with three contracts worth millions of US dollars. 'The obvious', as I understood it, was only a matter of joining the dots.

And then he ended up dead on the road to Bagram. Pretty weird. Who knows—it might have been the Taliban.

The FBI, as it turned out, never closed the case and never found the perpetrators. John Allen got Junior's body and took it back to the States, but Four Horsemen didn't look after Junior's wife very well. It was a shit affair all round.

Junior dying didn't make me more scared. I was already resigned to the fact that I was probably going to die in prison. In a way, I didn't care about myself. Junior, on the other hand, had an awesome wife and a new child, a great future to live for. He was my friend, a really good guy who deserved better. He just wanted to go to another company where he was safer.

We had got ourselves mixed up with some bad people. In Afghanistan, I'd always expected that from the insurgency. I never anticipated how lethal were our enemies within.

PART TWO

PART TWO

The Seventh Circle of Hell

2010–2012

6

Punishment

In the jail at Tolkeef, the name 'Pol-e-Charkhi' was used as a dark threat. If you stepped out of line in any way, the guards would say 'You are going to Pol-e-Charkhi', and that was enough to quieten down any prisoner. It was spoken of as a fate worse than death. For decades, Pol-e-Charkhi had been Afghanistan's centre of government torture and murder. A mass grave from the Russian era unearthed more than two thousand bodies there. In 2007, the Americans renovated it a little, so that they could move in hardcore Al-Qaeda and Taliban prisoners who had previously been in Guantanamo Bay.

Two days after I received the death sentence at my five-minute court hearing, I was sent to Pol-e-Charkhi for the first time. Once prisoners had been sentenced it was standard procedure to move them out of Tolkeef, which was a remand centre, to one of the wings at Pol-e-Charkhi.

Pol-e-Charkhi was on the outskirts of Kabul, in the desert, close to Black Horse, an American training area for the Afghan army. The prison was built in the shape of a wheel with twelve spokes or separate numbered blocks, each two to four storeys high.

Block 7 of Pol-e-Charkhi, where I was dumped, was like some seventh circle of hell, Dante Alighieri's place of ultimate suffering. But it's not easy to describe, or to render the full experience of what it was like there. I had no external perspective: I was taken there inside a dark bumping police van, and when I came out I was inside a building. It wasn't until a year or so later that I even saw the place from the outside.

This disorientation was part of the mind-fuck. I was not physically tortured or brutalised, or no more than I had been already. The thing about it was that they just locked you up in a bare concrete cell without any food or water. The core of Afghan ruthlessness was this negligence. I'm not even sure if any of it was deliberate so much as incompetent. Instead of beating you, they just dumped you and forgot you, like you were rubbish. You became invisible to them, and in some dark and horrifying way, you became invisible to yourself. Forgotten, you ceased to exist. You didn't know from one hour to the next whether this was where you would die. They put you in there to destroy your mind.

The cell was six feet by eight feet, with a barred wall on one side looking out onto a narrow corridor. In the opposite wall of the cell was a small ventilation hole that connected into a shaft that ran up the centre of the building. The dominant smell in the cell was from rubbish and rotting food that had been shoved into that shaft. People had thought if they shoved leftover rubbish through the hole and into the shaft it became someone else's problem. Instead, it reeked like you were living in a tip, and the stench became every-body's problem.

As in Tolkeef, there was a constant noise of Afghans, the other prisoners, talking and shouting from cell to cell. The guards were rarely there. They locked the place up and went off to get stoned, leaving it to the prisoners to run. There was a riot in Block 7 while I was there, and the way the police dealt with it was to do nothing, just lock the doors and let the inmates sort it out like *Lord of the Flies*. Once it settled down, the police found a body in there, a prisoner who they had thought was in another block. Some of the prisoners had paid the guards to bring him over there as a rent boy, and he was murdered.

Certain prisoners were given the job to feed other prison-ers, and the first time I was in Block 7, I was fed by a Pakistani who was all right. But because I wasn't a Muslim, I wasn't let out of my cell at prayer or regular meal times, and occasion-ally they wouldn't let me out when I needed to go to the toilet.

There was no toilet that worked in the cell, only a squat toilet down the corridor. I asked again and again to go, but often they refused. I didn't want to stink out my cell by pissing or shitting, so I held it in. That was hard, but eventually that first Pakistani was merciful enough to let me go, or I could go during the one hour of exercise I was allowed every few days. I was also dehydrated. While I was in the exercise area, a triangular yard slightly bigger than a tennis court, I looked in the rubbish that was lying around everywhere and found a discarded plastic bottle. I took that to the toilet and tried to fill it from the wash basin. Usually no water came out of the tap, but I was lucky this time and could fill up my water bottle and take it back to the cell.

It was a rough ten days. Normally I was okay with being isolated, but the uncertainty played tricks with my mind.

I didn't know what was going on or how long it would last. I couldn't get in touch with anyone, and no one knew where I was. The punishment wasn't the physical deprivation, but thinking I was lost in the system. They could kill me, I thought, and nobody would know. They really didn't care, they had no empathy for other people, life meant nothing. I was thinking, I'm going to die here, and they'll just say, 'Oh yeah, he died.' Nothing more.

Before I became confused and disoriented, I was pissed off, more than anything, at the thought of dying in there. It's not a good way to die, locked in a cold stone room. I'd never imagined my life ending this way. When I got to that point, I almost gave up. Then I tried to talk myself into fantasies of resistance. *They're going to come and bash me. If they're going to do it, they're going to do it. But when they come, there'd better be more than one of them.*

Yet they never came, which, in an unnerving way, was even worse.

During those days in Block 7, I was a space cadet, barely rational or able to take in information. A young Hazara translator working with the Australian embassy came in and told me they would move me out of Pol-e-Charkhi and back to Tolkeef in a couple of days. I didn't even know where I was. Glen, accompanied by Marcus Wilson, came to visit me while I was in the block, and continued promising he would do something for me. Glen stayed in Afghanistan for some months longer, but that was the last time I saw him. The next time I spoke to him was on the phone, and I wasn't feeling so warm and fuzzy about him anymore. He said, 'I need more money, we'll sort it all out.' I said no. I never saw or heard from him again.

The reason I was taken back to Tolkeef after ten days was

that Leanne from the Australian embassy had come to visit, only to be told that I was in Pol-e-Charkhi. Because it was an hour out of town, the trip to Pol-e-Charkhi was deemed unsafe for Australian embassy staff, so the prison authorities agreed to drive me back and keep me in Room 1 at Tolkeef for the duration of my legal case, which I vaguely understood could run for another couple of months. So I was taken back to Tolkeef, badly rattled by my time in Block 7. From then on, the threat of it was hanging over me constantly. Any misstep in Tolkeef, they only had to mention Pol-e-Charkhi or 'the punishment block', and I would freak out. I was terrified of it, the first time I felt real marrow-deep fear.

Within weeks, my nightmare came true.

———

Because I was on my own, prisoners would often try it on, assaulting me for no other reason than boredom. During evening prayers, the guards let me out to walk in the hallway. That was my only time out of the room really, when the Afghans were too busy to bother me. I snatched a few minutes of peace and quiet. Well, peace anyway. There was a wannabe Taliban guy who ran his finger across his throat whenever he walked past me. I grew sick of it and got into a fight with him in the toilet. He didn't do me any damage, but it did cause some shit again.

This time the guards decided to punish me physically, hanging me up against a wall in the stress position, wrists tied above my head, while they and some of the prisoners stood staring at me and gibbering among themselves. For whatever reason, they decided not to get too physical, as they did to a mentally disabled Afghan who, while he was hanging on the wall, had lit matches and cigarette butts thrown at him. They brought his food up to his face and then dropped it on the ground. They would poke him with brooms and batons. He screamed and screamed at them, and still they wouldn't stop. I guess I could count myself lucky to have escaped that.

I didn't escape Block 7, though. The next day they sent me back there.

The wannabe Talib shithead who had attacked me had also been sent to Block 7, and I had a score to settle with him. The next time the cell doors were open for afternoon exercise, I waited until he went to the toilet and then followed him. He was taking a piss, squatting down in the Afghan style. I went up and kicked him as hard as I could in the face. I left him there and went back to my cell. I never had a problem with him after that.

The second time I was in Block 7, the prisoner who fed me was again a Pakistani, but unlike the first one he was a nasty piece of work. When he came to my door, he said he would feed me. I said great. He said, 'But only if you convert to Islam.' The pressure to convert had been bubbling along in the prison system from the word go, and I had seen how quickly Glen let himself be drawn into it, but here they turned it into an art form.

'No,' I said.

'Why?'

'Because I don't believe in it. I don't believe in any religion. I've killed enough people to know that there's no God there. Fuck, you people are proof of that.'

That didn't go down so well; no dinner for me that night.

His other way of expressing his dislike for me was to flat-out refuse my requests to go to the toilet. In the end, I was bursting so badly, I pissed through the bars into the hallway.

He went off, shouting and screaming and calling the guards. When they came and asked me why I pissed in the hallway, I said, 'I did it because he wouldn't let me out.' The guards turned to the Pakistani guy and said he had to let me out to go to the toilet, even if I wasn't a Muslim. So I went. But if I thought I had been given a reprieve, I was wrong. When I came back to my cell, the Pakistani gave me tea. But he or the guards must have slipped Valium or some other heavy tranquilliser into it, because it laid me out cold for the best part of three days. I didn't cause him any problems for that period.

———

I don't know how many days I'd been back in Block 7 before the hallucinations started.

A mate of mine from the battalion, Chris 'Camel' Ahmelman, came in and had a chat to me for a few hours.

'Listen,' he said, 'you're better than this. You're better than any of these pricks.'

'But you're dead, mate,' I replied aloud. 'You're not here.'

'Yeah, I know,' he said. 'But I'm here now.' And he was: I could see him.

Camel died when we were in Iraq, back in 2005. He was working for Edinburgh International, the same as me, but on a different project. He was on Apollo, protecting the interim Iraqi government while also training up their local boys for the long term. I was on Artemis, a USAID contract, looking after the people setting up and overseeing the elections.

On 20 April, we were on the way back from an airport run along the infamous Route Irish, me as the gunner in the boss's car at the rear of the convoy. As we sped along, I noticed stationary traffic on the other side of the freeway. An

IED (improvised explosive device) had been found by the US military and they had pushed the traffic well back while they cleared it. I recognised the motley collection of vehicles pushing through the Iraqis and trying to get the attention of the soldiers with a marker panel. Rob B, my boss, said from the passenger seat, 'Rob, is that the Apollo callsign on the left?'

'Roger, friendly callsign static left,' I said. 'Looks like they're trying to get past the Yanks.'

Fifteen minutes later we were back in our street in the Green Zone and were halfway through the debrief when Rob B took a phone call. He grabbed JT, the 2IC on the project, and had a quick word, before taking off for the company Ops Room down the street. JT said, 'Gear on, lads, back in the cars—Apollo is in contact where we passed them. The boss is just grabbing the details, then we're gone.'

As I threw on my vest, JT shook his head and said, 'Not you, Robbie mate. You stay here.'

I knew then that something had happened to Camel. As I was still a relative unknown on Rob B's team, he wasn't going to risk me flipping out during the recovery and risking more lives. Fair enough. In the end we lost three guys: Camel, Steph and Kyle. Enough has been written about that contact, good and bad, so I won't go into it. The video taken from inside Camel's car was still up on YouTube when I looked twelve years later.

Camel, who was a sniper, and I got to know each other back in Townsville when I was first in the army. About a year older than me, he had done the tour in Somalia with 1RAR. In the mid-1990s, after thinking about becoming an officer in the army, he left to go into private work. Having got a bit of money together in Iraq, he was preparing to go to South Africa to do the same Close Protection course

I'd done, and then was going to come over to the Artemis project. The Apollo project would be finishing up sooner than ours and Rob B, being one of the company owners, was keen to keep good guys around.

We had a good old chat in Pol-e-Charkhi, catching up on what had happened during the four years since his death.

I look at it now and I think I know why hallucinations like that happen. I don't believe in ghosts or magic or muti or any of that shit. I think your brain resets and configures information in a way that's going to help you survive. Under the pressure of ten days in solitary confinement, you can snap, but sometimes your brain can manage to snap in a way that's going to benefit you. You hallucinate so that you can process things. Camel's death had affected me in ways that I had not acknowledged or dug down into. But probably he was the closest person to me, before I went to Afghanistan, who had lost his life. For four years, I'd locked him away, and now it was no accident that he was coming back to me. Some part of my unconscious was telling me that there were things that were precious to me, things that were worth living for.

Seeing Camel was also, in some way, a message from the 1RAR mafia. They were, as they had been since I was a seventeen-year-old, my second family. During my years in jail, blokes I knew from my time in the battalion would come in and slip me some money or food or offer to make calls and organise something for me. They knew I would do the same for them.

In the weeks after Glen got out and stabbed me in the back, two other mates from the 'Bn' stepped up to the plate.

Scotty and I were in 9 Platoon, C Company, back in the 1990s, and went together to East Timor on 1RAR's tour in 2000–01. After I left the army in 2004, Scotty, a fellow South

Australian, went to the Battalion Sniper Cell. Dave had been upstairs from us in the barracks, in 12 Platoon, D Company. Our bosses had been through the Royal Military College Duntroon together and shared a house out of town, and both platoons had a reputation of going hard in barracks or the bush. On a few occasions we had dual platoon piss-ups, calling ourselves the 9/12th Independent Rifle Company, referring to the World War II units who were left to their own devices in the Pacific with little command oversight and told to cause as much havoc among the Japanese until support came. We didn't fight many Japanese, but we caused plenty of havoc.

By 2009, Scotty and Dave were both working as private security contractors in Afghanistan. Dave had started at Global and worked at the UK embassy with Jon Goodman before he and Scotty set up their own business doing security for a helicopter company.

In the year I'd been working in Afghanistan, the three of us hung out together a fair bit. Scotty and Dave gave me light relief from all the bullshit going on at Four Horsemen, and it was normal anyway for blokes from the Bn who hadn't seen each other for years to reconnect in faraway places after moving into private companies, or even if some of them had moved to other parts of the Australian military. We knew to look after each other. When I was in jail, Scotty and Dave channelled donations of money and food from other ex-1RAR guys in country, and Scotty got a dive bag, backpack and a box of my personal possessions back from Four Horsemen. Needless to say, it had been picked over pretty well by the time Scotty got it. None of my Ops gear, computers, Rolex or my leather jacket remained. Any old crap had been shoved in in its place. Afterwards, this gear went into the Q-store run by the various security companies that held the Australian embassy contract over the seven years. I got the half-full dive bag back and nothing else. When people think you're not coming out, they can do some shit things.

After the Glen debacle, Scotty and Dave were my main link with the outside world until they left Afghanistan in 2012. That would amount to nearly three years of bringing me money, clothes and food; passing messages and smoothing things over with the embassy or anyone else; or putting pressure on Four Horsemen to honour their responsibilities to someone they had left in jail.

My army mates became all-important in mid-2010 when the embassy staff weren't able to visit as much. In those months, I was being bounced between Tolkeef and the punishment wing at Pol-e-Charkhi before I was moved to Pol-e-Charkhi for good. The various companies that held the Australian embassy security contract in Kabul changed a few times over the years, all having a different take on risk management. The security staff were essentially all the same, just moving from one company to another. Ivan stuck with the contract right up to 2016, so there was some continuity. In situations like this you find out who your true mates are.

————

My second court hearing came up in the winter of 2009 to 2010. This time, I was a bit better prepared than I had been for the first. I was hoping I would be able to speak up on my own account, and prepared myself thoroughly.

The second hearing was again in an office, albeit a bigger one, because this was the Supreme Court. Once more, my lawyer Bashir was late, and so was my interpreter. Jeremy Kelly was there. By then, he was harassing me about my family, wanting to do a story with them. I said, 'Stay the fuck away from them.' Sure enough, a few weeks later he turned up at my family's house in Port Augusta. The whole town closed ranks on him. Joy Baluch, the mayor and also the mother of a friend of my sister's husband (small town, I know), told the media that if they kept annoying our family they should get the fuck out of town. Jeremy Kelly's approach particularly upset Dad, and I did not appreciate his harassment of a vulnerable elderly man.

I again asked for Kelly to be removed from the court, but my request was knocked back. Presently, Bashir turned up and things got rolling. A prosecuting attorney began to ask some questions about the shooting of Karim Abdullah. They were relying on the statement from the Nepalese contractor, Chandra Singh Butt, who had been with us that night. I pointed out that Butt had been asleep at the time of the incident. The prosecutor asked me to accept my crime 'which was as clear as the sun'. I said no, I had shot Karim in self-defence because he had put his pistol in my face.

'Why didn't you run away?'

'It's not my job to run away.'

'Why didn't you shoot him in the leg?'

'It's a lot harder than you think in that situation to shoot someone in the leg.'

'Why didn't you fire a warning shot?'

Even though I'd promised myself to stay calm, I did burr up at the stupidity of some of the questions. I understood that in the Middle East it was commonplace for police and military to fire in the air to get people's attention, but I'd found myself to be in a life-and-death situation, with a pistol aimed at me in the middle of an angry argument. Almost twenty years of experience took over and I'd neutralised the threat without even thinking. It's what soldiers are trained to do. At one point, I went on a bit of a rant, at the end of which I told my interpreter, 'And tell him that.'

With which the interpreter said about three words.

Bashir was no better. Whenever he tried to speak, the judge shut him up with a curt, 'We don't want to know.'

'Oh, okay,' Bashir said, sitting down.

Luckily, I had Scotty and Dave there to handle him, by which I mean, refuse his ridiculous demands for bribes. Outside the court room during a break, Bashir suggested that a few thousand dollars could make a difference. In Afghanistan a few thousand dollars in the right place could be the difference between life and death. In the wrong place, they were just dollars thrown away. Scotty and Dave told Bashir to fuck right off.

The news came quickly after the hearing that they'd given me a death sentence again. The next morning I was sent back to the punishment block at Pol-e-Charkhi for six days. I hadn't paid the required bribe to stay in the VIP room at Tolkeef, so it was Block 7 for me. More isolation, more hallucinating, more horror. It was fucked. The embassy argued to get me out. Eventually I got back in the VIP room, where I learnt that Four Horsemen had now made a final decision to break ties and stop sending me any food. Apparently John Allen had been made to feel guilty enough to send some supplies, but either he had left the country or his stock of guilt had run out.

That was a real kick in the teeth. Against the mounting evidence, I had still believed that John Allen was almost some superhuman being who would swoop down, understand everything that had gone wrong, and use his influence to pluck me out of jail and get me out of the country. Now that hope was gone, and I almost felt I was gone too. I would walk in circles in the yard feeling myself fall apart, like my actual arms and legs and head were coming loose and someone would find me in a little heap.

The months ground by. Day in and day out of doing nothing. The boredom sat against a constant backdrop of tension and violence that I did my best to avoid. Sometimes, however, attempting to keep out of trouble was interpreted by Afghans as fear. And that created a whole new set of problems.

In Tolkeef, we were allowed to shower once every two days. You had to buy your own hot water, hot enough to wash yourself or your clothes in. One of the shower days coincided with the 'shooter boys' being brought into the prison, when the guards rounded up young male sex workers on Thursdays, leaving them in the prison for three nights so that they could ply their trade among the inmates and also the guards themselves. Before I went for my shower, one of the boys was in the shower cubicle soliciting customers. When I got there, I told him in my best broken Dari to fuck off out of it. He began gobbing off at me, so I picked him up by his neck and pushed him out. As he went out the door, he tripped over my bucket of hot water, began screaming, and ran off. Ten minutes later there was a bang on the shower door, and rent-a-crowd was waiting for me.

'Righto,' I said, 'Let's have you then. Who's first?'

They said, 'No, you've got to go see the commandant.'

I went before the commandant of the prison, who strung me up by the wrists in a watch cell. I was still only wearing my towel.

'You assaulted this boy and poured boiling water over him,' the commandant said.

'No, he tripped over it when I threw him out the fucking door.'

This pointless to-and-fro went on for a while. The commandant suggested I could get dressed and go back to my cell if I paid him a bribe. I refused, and was left alone for a bit, then they allowed me to get dressed, before putting me in handcuff chains and leg irons. Some kind of investigation took place outside, and the next morning, after they took the chains and irons off, the commandant came in and said, 'You were right and the boy was wrong. But we're going to send you to Pol-e-Charki anyway, because you cause trouble.'

That commandant would end up in jail himself, for taking bribes. He got twenty years, served two, and went back into the police force. If you've served your time in Afghanistan, you can go back to your old job, even as a policeman, soldier or politician. With a uniform and connections, you can get away with anything.

He barked a few orders at his men and I was tied up in chains, put in a bus without any of my belongings, and driven to Pol-e-Charkhi for the last time. I just thought: *That's me then.*

7

Why I was there

John Allen had been the person who gave me the opportunity to break the cycle of despair that had been doing my head in. It was when John let me set up and run my own team that I began to find a purpose in my job. I had gone to Afghanistan with what amounted to a death wish, but that lifted during the second half of my year with Four Horsemen. I had John to thank for that.

The boss worked in mysterious ways. We would never know when he was coming into the country. He never told people what he was doing, which was good thinking, because he kept them all guessing. I didn't mind. He would email me and let me know stuff. After an incident near Kandahar in October 2008, about three months after I started with Four Horsemen, John took me into his confidence.

I'd started out in Afghanistan with the idea that John was just my boss. Tell me what to do and pay me, I don't give a rat's. But after a while, we clicked, and a lot of that had to do with a long trip we took to Kandahar.

Up to August 2008, I had done some small security trips outside Kabul with Americans from the company, and wasn't impressed at all with the way Four Horsemen did things. Then one day John said, 'Do you want to come on this heavy run down south? You can hang out in my vehicle.'

I was keen to see how he operated, and he evidently wanted to see how I performed under fire. The convoy had to go down a notorious strip of road south-west from Kabul through Ghazni towards the city that had always been the traditional Taliban stronghold. NATO wouldn't drive between Ghazni and Kandahar, even with full military protection. That's how risky it was.

We were escorting about one hundred fuel trucks into Helmand Province, and then further south into the Red Desert. The Americans were building a base pretty much wherever their helicopters found it safe to land and drop stuff off. If there was a degree of randomness to the Americans' and the Afghan government's planning, the insurgents on the other hand seemed well set-up. There were said to be well-organised, well-equipped Chechen insurgents waiting down there to pick off the convoys, while the Afghans were always on the look-out to grab some free fuel.

We began getting shot at before Salar, about halfway from Kabul to Kandahar, and were under fire pretty much the whole way from there. It was mental—like something out of *Mad Max II*. We were trying not to engage the shooters, but were forced to stop. This was just what they wanted, but an RPG round had smacked a hole in the side of one of our fuel trucks. We pulled over, and I was standing there thinking, *Holy fuck—it didn't go off?* There was a pin in the nose of the grenade that armed the firing mechanism, but fortunately the idiots hadn't taken it out. So the whole truck didn't explode—which was a good thing probably. The round, which was stuck in the side of the tank, had punched a hole in it, and fuel was pissing out everywhere. As I was poking about in the fuel truck, John was screaming at me, 'Get the fuck out of there!' But he didn't realise that if the truck hadn't exploded immediately, it wasn't going to now. An Afghan trucker came up, pulled the RPG round out, bunched together some old rags and wood, and knocked up a plug to fill the hole. Then tracer bullets began skimming off the road around us and I took cover, thinking, *What the fuck am I doing here again?*

We weren't much further down the road before a new group started firing on us. There were dickheads taking pot shots all the way along, but sometimes the fire was too heavy for us to just drive on through, and we had to answer back.

There was a guy shooting at us from about a kilometre away, making a real pest of himself. I took a gun out of our car: it was a Romanian PS1, which is like a Russian Dragonov sniper rifle but a much better weapon. John and I were lying on the shoulder of the road, looking at where the guy was firing from, and I was trying to work out how to use the scope.

'Have you ever fired one of these in combat?' John said.

'No, I haven't,' I said, 'but I'll give it a go.'

The retinal patterning the Russians used on their scopes was really easy to use, and John was telling me how to adjust it to pinpoint the target.

Looking at the numbers on the scope, I said, 'Is this in yards or metres?'

'I don't fucking know,' John said.

I replied, 'Aren't you the 18B?'

I thought, the Russians are European, so it's got to be metric. Then the guy fired at us again and the round bounced off the bonnet of the car.

John lost it and screamed in my ear: 'Shoot the cunt!'

'Yeah, sure,' I said, 'but I don't know what the fuck I'm doing. I reckon it's in metres.'

Then the guy fired another round that smashed into the car's armour plating. John was throwing a bit of a tantrum now.

'If you don't shoot that prick . . .!'

Right at that moment, I fired. Spot-on. I got the guy. Roughly 850 away—metres, I think.

'Whoa, that was awesome!' John said.

'Pure fluke, more like it.' But I was quietly pleased to have done something that he would remember.

We were in so many running battles that day, we ran out of ammunition. Later in the year, I would do that same trip, ensuring that I took lots of heavy weapons and ammo. My strategy was to blow the fuck out of anyone who hit us. We learnt how to do it fast: Kabul to Kandahar in eighteen hours. But this time, it took us two days. They were after the fuel. It wasn't just Taliban, it was people who wanted to steal and sell it. Great place for an Australian to be.

We kept going through the night, but more slowly, and were hit less than during the day. During these long drives, especially as you're winding down from one contact and on high alert for the next, you often exchange stories. John told me about the ambush he'd been in a couple of years earlier in Afghanistan, when he had lost his eyesight and part of his knee. Separated out the front of his convoy, he had got out of his vehicle to engage the guys who were firing on them.

An RPG round hit the ground and exploded a few metres away, launching John into the air so that he ended up on the bonnet of his car. The next RPG whistled in and hit the front of the car. The impact blew him back through the windscreen. He bounced right through the main cabin of the vehicle and landed in the tray. As he dragged himself out, the insurgents swept down from the hills and shot at him twice more. He got himself into a decent position and cleaned up those guys—but then he got shot again. He moved away from his vehicle; seconds later, it got blown up by another RPG around.

'That's all I remember,' he said. 'Next thing I know, I woke up in Germany, all fucked up.'

By rights, he should have been dead. 'When they saw the state of me, they thought I was going to die.' But he didn't. Tough motherfucker.

When we got further down into Helmand, we were hit again. There was a Polish army base nearby and they brought a vehicle, a KTO Rosomak, with a 30mm cannon, German-made, very powerful. They said, 'You go now!' We moved on, as ordered, and got a distant view of the Poles shooting the shit out of that bunch of insurgents.

Further south, it never relented. As the sun was setting on the second day, we lost a few of our Afghan guys when a round hit the vehicle of one of the commanders of our security team. It missed him, but his driver had the back of his head blown out. His face remained intact while his brain was in the back tray of the truck. We towed that vehicle out. The commander was moved to another vehicle, where two of his guys were killed, but somehow he survived again. He was a mental wreck, he'd been blown up that many times in an hour.

With so much damage to that team—the commander was immediately sent out of harm's way—we had to requisition a replacement security team from another province. Within a few hours, they wanted to quit. They were shitting themselves. We were now on the road to Lashkar Gah in Helmand, west of Kandahar, where the marijuana and opium crops were thick on the ground. We had a new type of enemy to deal with. For the farmers, the drug crop was their livelihood, so if they saw people with guns coming through, they would shoot at you. They weren't international Islamic radicals or Taliban; they just wanted us to fuck off. So before long we were getting shot at by them too. At one point we were lying in fields of marijuana up to two metres high, squashing the plants and rolling through them, getting high on the resin fumes.

Lashkar Gah is a Taliban city, with a complex terrain. They have a labyrinth of irrigation canals with culverts running under the roads, which were some of the insurgents' favourite places to set up an ambush or an IED. When we were going through, we got into a massive contact. I fell into a culvert and couldn't get out. I was shitting myself, waiting for rounds to come screaming down on me, trying to climb up the side of the culvert like an ant. We got up to the road just as some westerners appeared on British quad bikes: they were most likely UK Special Forces.

'You blokes look like you could do with some,' they said in that typical, super-capable but calm UKSF way.

We went to their small but very well set-up compound for a rest. We were smashed, trying to come down from what had been two days and nights of more or less non-stop fighting. But as comforting as it was to be in the company of the Brits, we had to get going again. At two or three o'clock in the morning, when things seemed to have calmed down, we headed off.

By daybreak, we got to the Red Desert. Our Afghans reckoned they knew where the base was, but the landscape was like Mars: literally a red desert, with no human construction anywhere in sight. We drove around in circles for the best part of the day, and when we eventually pulled up, we still hadn't found it. This was truly fucked. And that night, we got hit again. It might have looked like an empty desert, but there were still people bobbing up and having a go at us. Another of our people got killed, I'm not sure how, possibly shot by one of his own guys. We cleaned up the shooters, but by now, on the whole trip, we had lost ten of our own men.

The next morning, the fatigue and stress caught up with us. I'd had a gutful of it and just wanted to curl up and sleep. We'd been nearly killed time after time, and now we could not find the bloody destination. I didn't know whether to laugh or cry. But then, alarmingly, John had a crisis of his own. He suffered from epilepsy as a result of the traumatic brain injuries he had undergone in battle, and had run out of his meds. Right there in the Red Desert, he had a full-blown fit. A couple of us had to hold him down until it passed through him. I just wanted to get him somewhere with medical help. Essentially, he was my client, as well as my boss. My job was to protect him above everything else. I had solid military medic's training behind me, but was not a paramedic. I didn't have the skills or medication to stabilise him to the point where he might not suffer another fit.

'Fuck this,' I said, and put the coordinates of the camp into my GPS. 'Right, we're going that way.'

After about three more hours of driving, I saw something grey on the horizon. We got closer. The greyness was Hesco barriers. A couple of Marine helicopter rotors were poking above them. The base. The fucking shitting base. Well, that was easy.

But that trip wouldn't have been complete without one last shot. When we got to the base, we noticed that British Army artillery were guarding it. As we approached the front, we saw a machine gun, but it was unmanned. I saw a pair of boots poking out from under it. The gunner was having a nap.

I threw a rock at his boots to give him a wake-up. He got a big fright. He jumped up and fired a flare at us. John, in his fragile state, went totally ballistic at him. To me, he said, 'Let's go round the other side, where fucking US Marines are guarding it.' It was quite funny in the circumstances. But not really. To cop a British flare in the face, after what we'd been through, would have been a less than dignified way to make our delivery.

We emptied the trucks into the fuel depots, turned around and drove all the way to Kandahar. Aside from getting shot up once by the drug farmers around Lashkar Gah, we copped nothing else. Amazing how they knew whether fuel trucks were full or empty.

Between Kandahar and Kabul, when we came to the area where our Afghan had been shot in the face, the drivers suddenly got cold feet and were reluctant to proceed, even with empty trucks. That's when I saw another side to John. He got out of the car, climbed onto the bonnet, and began pole dancing around the HF aerial. He looked like a fucking lunatic, and I didn't know whether to leave him there or drag him in. But there was a method to his madness. When the Afghans saw him dancing around like this, they started cheering and laughing. He was showing them that there was nothing to worry about here. When he hopped back into our car and we started off, at the head of the convoy, the trucks followed.

'You've got to understand the way they think,' he said. 'If I'm the biggest swinging dick and I'm treating this area like it's a joke, they'll all follow me.'

When we were on our way back, we came across a camp of Pashtuns doing security for a road building project. It was the same spot where we'd been hit on the way out. This guy with a long beard came out to meet us. Through our interpreter, the guy told John he was sick of stationary security work and wanted to travel around more. Basically, he hit John up for a job. I looked at him and said to John, 'Hang on, aren't these the guys who attacked us a couple of days ago?'

John and the Pashtun leader talked for about fifteen minutes. Commander Mansour was in his late twenties or early thirties and looked like an Afghan version of Jesus: long hair, trimmed beard, very chilled in his demeanour. In fact, he acted like he was permanently stoned, though I don't think he was. He had fought for the Northern Alliance with his brother since they were young. He introduced us to his brother, who had a skewiff eye and reminded me of the Cookie Monster. He'd got blown up by a Russian mine while they were playing as kids. He was calm up to a point, but would then lose the plot with people. Still, their gang respected him. If they fucked up, he would pull them into line.

Mansour's request to work for John would have been a bit of a shock anywhere else but in Afghanistan. Most of the population really were mercenaries. They would work for whoever they respected, who would pay and look after them. The Taliban used mercenaries all the time, and most of Mansour's guys had worked for their fellow Pashtuns in the Taliban at one stage or another.

It had been a bad trip. We had lost ten Afghan security guys: bad by any measure. It was also the first fighting of that magnitude that I had been in in my life. I had been in plenty of smaller encounters, but nothing like this. To me it had never felt out of control, and that was reassuring. This was what I was trained to do and what I had taught others to do. It was very interesting to experience it first-hand and find that for me the processes of combat were as natural as breathing. I'd always felt that I would do well, but you can't really know for sure until you do it.

Without doubt, those days forged my relationship with John. He saw how I was with the Afghans. As a Green Beret, he had been raised on the idea that to make things possible in foreign lands, you have to respect local cultures. He liked that I treated the Afghans as partners. And he knew now that I wasn't like the rest of the guys in the company. He saw what I was like under fire, that it didn't faze me. I might not have cared about my own survival as much as others did. I didn't care about a lot of things, but on the field of battle, that trans- lated into a kind of courage.

Now was the time to speak. 'I want to do things my own way,' I told him. I didn't trust Haussedin and his Panjshiri heavies, and I wasn't happy reporting to the Macedonians on daily operations. The less I had to do with Kyle the better. When we got back to Kabul, I outlined a plan to John: I wanted to run my own crew of Afghans based in Ghazni rather than Kabul. I wanted to use Pashtun rather than Panjshiri security: I asked if I could build a team from Commander Mansour and his guys.

John said that they would be a good group for me to work with if I wanted to run things separately from the Panjshiris. I trusted the Pashtuns not because they were great people but because I would pay them more than they were currently getting. There was a different language that applied here, not what you expect from your armchair in Australia or the USA. After we had handed their arses to them, Mansour said, they wanted to work on our side. Application of force is the thing they respect, and unless they see it themselves they don't believe it.

Essentially, I wanted to be able to spend what was necessary on weaponry to get a convoy through the kind of fight we had just been through. I was all about being effective, not making myself popular with the office or greasing the situation for personal profit.

John agreed: I could do things my own way. Over the next month, he turned me around and gave me a positive reason for being in Afghanistan.

John and I cemented the kind of work friendship that possibly only comes about through sharing the experience we'd had, under fire, where we could die at any minute. He became a real mentor to me. I had come to Afghanistan at a low point, but everything changed after that long trip. I had always respected John, and now I felt that it was mutual.

When he was in country, John asked me to act as his personal bodyguard. This made for some interesting sights and conversations.

I escorted him to meetings with General David Petraeus, the head of the US forces in Afghanistan, as well as other senior western generals. I was with him when he went to meet Abdul Rashid Dostum, the war lord who had been the most powerful person in Afghanistan since the 1980s—and, in my opinion, an out-and-out lunatic.

Dostum, who came from Uzbekistan, had commanded a huge militia in the north of Afghanistan when the Russians

occupied the country. He was a collaborator, suppress-
ing the mujahideen in the north and fighting on the side
of the Russians' puppet president, Najibullah. After the
Russians pulled out, Dostum switched sides, helping Shah
Massoud and the Northern Alliance overthrow the Najibullah government. But after that, during the four years of
civil war and instability between 1992 and the rise of the
Taliban, Dostum changed sides again, fighting against
Massoud.

The only time Dostum had lost influence in the country
was when the Taliban took over in 1998. He fled to Turkey,
where he hid out until the Americans marched in in October
2001. Then he was back, and ever since then, he had increased
his influence in the north while the Americans turned a blind
eye to his excesses, which included a long series of massa-
cres and murders. When Hamid Karzai became president in
2003, under American protection, Dostum became a deputy
defence minister and ruled the north, though after an assassination attempt he spent a lot of that time back in Turkey.
Karzai was terrified of him, John told me, but needed him to
keep order in the north.

John knew Dostum from the old days—there was always
some murky connection in John's past—and we went to his
compound for a week while the pair of them did 'business'.
Dostum was a bearlike, heavy-set guy in his sixties with short
grey hair and a drooping black moustache, permanently in
military uniform and surrounded by dozens of guards.

The first shock for me was seeing tanks in his backyard.
He really did command his own army. There were plenty
of war lords in Afghanistan, most of them tinpot pseudo-
dictators like Haussedin, but Dostum was clearly operating
at a different level. To have armaments of this size, in the

backyard of his house, was a display that he was as powerful as a nation in himself.

It was a bit sketchy why John was there. He didn't fill me in on the details, he just wanted me with him for security. I wasn't in the room to observe their business. They had some big feeds together, sometimes in a group, other times just John and Dostum and a terp in a room while I was standing outside looking at the tanks. There were other war lords who turned up at the house. Some days, a bunch of Taliban leaders would show up and go inside to do business. This was another shock. But I learnt that the Taliban were getting paid by the US government, through Four Horsemen, to stop blowing Americans up. This must have been one of the deals being done between John and Dostum: protection money passed by the US, through John, to Dostum, and on to the Taliban. The deal was simple: 'How much money do you want to stop killing our people?' The Taliban named their price, and we were paying them in big envelopes John carried, stuffed with forty or fifty grand in US dollars. Even at the highest levels, this whole thing was a racket.

Dostum was completely illiterate, John told me, but he had a good head on his shoulders for strategic thinking. That said, he was a mental case. John told me about an incident in the early days of the war against the Taliban when a group of prisoners had been put into shipping containers by Dostum's militia. John had been part of the Special Forces team who were advising them. One day, he told me, Dostum had too many whiskeys and decided to put 'breathing holes' in the shipping containers while prisoners were inside. He did it with a DShK 12.7mm machine gun. Later, while I was in jail, Afghan President Ashraf Ghani sent Dostum down to Helmand to take control of the struggling government forces, and everyone rallied behind the big dog. His militia were cutting off heads and leaving them alongside the road. For brutality, Dostum's militia was as bad as ISIS. President Ghani just let it slide.

Among John's many old acquaintances were some of the wildest and most enigmatic characters of the whole war. One was an infamous American dude called Jack Idema. Much about Idema was myth—of his own making—but according to John, he was ex-7th Special Forces, and went to Afghanistan in early 2002 off his own bat to start bounty hunting Taliban. He was working with Haussedin when he was caught running a private prison in 2004. In the wake of the Abu Ghraib business in Iraq, the Americans became very jumpy, in public at least, about prison abuse and torture. Idema put Haussedin's nose out of joint in some way, and was arrested in mid-2004 when Afghan police found eight men hanging from their feet and wearing hoods in Idema's prison.

Idema claimed he was operating with official approval, which the Pentagon denied. He became the first westerner to be thrown into Pol-e-Charkhi. They sentenced him to ten years, but he was out within three. By the time I was in the prison, Jack had gone off to run a tourism business in Mexico, where he died of AIDS in 2012.

John's shadiest links were with the Afghan police and government. A couple of times, I went with him to meet a police general called Ali Shah Paktiawal, who I saw as just another crooked cop without realising the extent of it. He'd worked alongside John in 2002, when John was attached to the CIA, and they were running black prisons in Kabul. Paktiawal was basically a thug, arresting whoever he wanted for the fun of it and demanding bribes to let them out. He walked around with a 9mm Smith & Wesson and liked to be known as 'the James Bond of Kabul'—though I can't see anyone casting, as the next Bond, a fat unhealthy middle-aged Afghan with a thin comb-over and a scuzzy moustache. His stock in trade was kidnapping pure and simple, and American intelligence and the US military let it happen. The *Financial Times* got onto his trail, discovering that he had millions of dollars' worth of property in Dubai, accumulated through ransom money. The paper said 'Kabul's top cop is also one of its top criminals'. This was the type of client John was happy to take on.

In September 2008, when I was John's bodyguard, there was a Taliban bomb attempt on the Paktiawal's life. Some people within his own government told the Taliban where he was going to be. The assassination attempt failed, but the next thing I knew Paktiawal had rocked up at the Four Horsemen compound with his entire family. John pulled me aside and said, 'I need you to run the road ahead of them up to Jalalabad. Junior's going to take them up to the border with Pakistan.'

I said, 'That's cool, I'm going that way for a job anyway.' My terp Mohammed and I went out and got through it all. We told John there were no police checkpoints before Jalalabad, which was what he wanted to know.

So we got Paktiawal out of the country. It wasn't until later that I found out he had been mixed up in drug smuggling, people smuggling, kidnapping and demanding protection money from whole towns. He was an out-and-out crim. Years later, when I got to know Taliban insiders in prison, I found out that the assassination attempt occurred after Paktiawal's own people found out he wasn't sharing the money with them. It was they who told the Taliban how to take him out. Pity the bomb missed its target.

It still intrigues me how John was mixed up with these people, but I was not naïve about what it took to do business in Afghanistan for a man of John's interests and background. Nobody was clean, yet I thought there could be a better way. I had long conversations with John about it, particularly when it came to corruption within the walls of his own company.

Our finance guy was a Kenyan who'd had a long association with Kyle. He was dodgy as fuck. I had to pay Afghans for the fuel we used, and if my books didn't work out he would just make up an inflated number and pocket the difference. I was used to this kind of thing, but he crossed the line when he asked John Allen to fund an orphanage he was claiming to set up in Kenya.

'Are you serious?' I said when John told me he had agreed. 'That's the oldest trick in the book. Oprah Winfrey got stung by that one for two million bucks in South Africa! They do it all the time: hire a building, hire street kids to act like happy orphans, take photos of them, and then tell them to fuck off.'

But John was adamant. 'I've been to Kenya and I've seen it.'

'You've seen the orphanage with your own eyes?'

John looked a bit shifty. 'Well, Ferozan has been over and seen it.' Ferozan was an Afghan woman who worked for the company, with whom John was having an affair. Her father was also doing things for Four Horsemen. As far as I was concerned, they were both milking John.

I said, 'Dude, do you want me to go over there and check it out?'

'It really is legit, Rob,' he said, before pulling up some photos to show me.

It was probably bullshit. The finance guy ripped John off repeatedly, but I could never convince him. I just couldn't work out why John let it happen. And why he let so much shit involving Haussedin and the likes of Paktiawal go on under his nose. I went to jail still holding on to this naïve belief about John, that he was deceived by these people. It wasn't until I was locked up that I realised that the face John showed me, solid and capable and competent and upstanding, was not the only face he had.

––––––––

Afghanistan was teaching me something about myself. I went there half expecting to get myself killed, but I have an interest bordering on obsessiveness in completing a job the right way.

After the hellish trip to Kandahar, when I asked John for autonomy to run convoy protection my own way, I built my team from the ground up. First, I needed a vehicle. I got my hands on an old Toyota Surf that had been sent to Afghanistan from Japan. It was probably stolen and wasn't in shape for civilian use, but it ran really well, with plenty of guts. I ripped out the back seats so that I could rack ammunition and the RPG launcher I carried. I had compartments to stash all sorts of stuff: phones, phone jammers, my laptop with a special mapping program, documents, and plenty of other gear I bought out of my own pocket. That car was great. Unfortunately, later in the year, while I went to Dubai for a meeting with John Allen, somebody borrowed it and crashed it. I got another Surf and fitted it out the same way.

Next was a driver and interpreter I trusted. I chose Mohammed, a Hazara who got on well with everybody.

At first, I was worried that he was a bit too charming, and I made sure to keep an eye on him. But he was terrific.

The next challenge was going outside Haussedin's Panjshiris to build a team, and this was the most controversial thing I did. I'd had the idea, after our initial meeting near Ghazni, to combine with Commander Mansour and his team. He came to Kabul and we hammered out a deal. His crew would stay at their base in Ghazni, on the road from Kabul to Kandahar, and stay well away from Haussedin's men. As Pashtuns, Mansour and his boys were sworn enemies of the Panjshiris anyway. If I was doing a job coming out of Kabul, they would wait for me at Maidan Shar, the last outpost before bandit country. I would, in time, trust them enough to keep some of my heavy weaponry and ammunition with them. Amazingly, before long I trusted these Pashtuns more than my own company. Mansour's boys looked up to him, and after we had done a few jobs, they looked up to me.

My team consisted of about thirty guys. All I had to do was pay Mansour directly, and he divided it up. I didn't get in the way of that.

In our fleet of vehicles, nobody but Mohammed and I got into my Toyota Surf. It was off-limits. Depending on what our job was, we also ran four or five gun trucks, each one a trayback Toyota LandCruiser with powerful Russian weapons: either a DShK 12.7mm machine gun, a 90mm SPG-9 recoilless rifle or an AGS-17 grenade launcher. Every truck had a machine gunner, a man with an RPG, and another with an AK. We had a lot of firepower. That was the idea—if we ran into any trouble with insurgents, we would blow the fuck out of them.

John Allen was happy for me to set myself up this way, and I could be effective. My biggest problems were with internal Four Horsemen politics. My new status put a few noses out of joint. The Macedonians were used to running jobs on the easiest route, from Kabul to Jalalabad, which was completely secure. I'd done it literally by myself, no problem at all. But still they complained that I suddenly had better money and more autonomy. It was wrong, they complained, because they had been there longer.

Petar and his mob were also pissed about the fact that John allowed me to do other jobs, outside of Four Horsemen, if I had nothing else on. I looked after a rep from Smith & Wesson, cash in hand. The Macedonians were jealous, but I was a professional. They were as free as I was to get freelance work during quiet times, but they were thugs with guns who couldn't get a job anywhere else.

Now that I had my own team, I had to keep an even closer eye on Haussedin. Because he controlled security at big American camps inside and outside Kabul, he knew what was going on all the time. Rather than confront him, I tried to outwit him. I told people I was going to one place and then went somewhere else with Mohammed. Panjshiri spies would get tired of watching for me and go home. Then I would go where I wanted, when there were no eyes around. I used to change it up all the time. Within Four Horsemen, I informed only John and Junior about my movements.

It may seem strange, then, that I trusted Afghan mercenaries who had previously worked for the Taliban. But I did not feel I was running an undue risk by throwing in my lot with Mansour, and it did not mean that I was in any way friendly towards the insurgency, who, after all, were the ones trying to smack us and our convoys. They remained our enemy. After we had done a run, my guys and I used to go to a restaurant outside Kandahar. A couple of times there were Taliban inside. I would walk in ahead of my crew and freak everybody out. The Taliban would be sitting there wearing their turbans, with AKs by their side. I'd walk in, all kitted up, and say, 'G'day, how ya going?' They would mutter away and then get on their motorbikes and leave. I knew I was safe: a restaurant in Afghanistan is essentially someone's house, and there was a respect for that even among enemies. The Taliban also knew that I had cars outside with 50-calibre weapons mounted on them. In a fight, that beats a shitty motorbike and an AK any day of the week. So they would slink away, and we could get on with our meal.

When I got to do the convoy protection my way, it actually became good fun. Truck drivers recognised me and called my name and I went off to eat with them, most of them showing themselves to be really good guys, not the dogsbodies and expendables the Macedonians and Panjshiris took them for. It was a big deal for them to have a westerner eat with them, especially if they were tribal Afghans. Sharing food is important for people who don't have much, and I was honoured to be their guest.

But they needed my help. They were having to pay back-handers everywhere. When they started listing the security teams they had to bribe, I thought, *Hang on, that guy's already getting paid by us.* So I told the drivers to tell them to fuck off. The corrupt security guards were pissed off with me for telling the drivers, but I stood firm. I said to the drivers, 'If you've got any problems with these people, just tell me. I'll sort it out.' So they went back to these corrupt idiots and said, 'The painted guy will shoot you.'

My appearance also made me a target. The Taliban believed that anyone with a painted rifle and a beard was

Special Forces or CIA, so they would shoot at us and try to get some good footage to use for propaganda use. No doubt my body strung across the front of one of their cars would be as attention-grabbing as the head of an SF soldier.

But I enjoyed hearing stories about the 'painted guy', sometimes 'the painted dog', which they called me on account of my tattoos. Back when I was in the Australian Army, I sketched my own tattoo designs and started getting some on my arms and chest. When I was in Cape Town in 2005, on a break from Iraq, I met Manuela Gray, a rock-star tattooist who had two shops and a studio there as well as a shop in London. I handed her the sketches and she gave me some eye-catching ink. The Afghans were fascinated by these tattoos. It was nice to be feared, but really awesome to be depended on. When it comes down to it, most workers in Afghanistan don't give a fuck about religion or politics, they want to feed their families and watch their kids grow up. If you can help just one person, that's a good start. Those drivers were risking their lives day after day for a couple of hundred bucks. They were just trying to earn a crust for their families, and were having bribes demanded all the time. If I could help them out by keeping some of their hard-earned from leaking out of their pockets, then I was making their families' lives a bit easier.

Deep down I began to think, for the first time in a long time, *Maybe I do have something to offer the world.* I had found my mojo again. With Mansour's team, we were doing good things, and we were doing them better than others. It was dangerous but satisfying work. If there was any one incident that epitomised what I feel I contributed and what motivated me to keep going, it was a contact in November 2008, at the onset of winter.

We were escorting two small trucks from Ghazni to Kabul. The truck drivers were good guys, and I had worked with one of them several times before. Their single connex containers were empty, having delivered US mail. US Postal Service mail from Bagram to the FOBs through Afghanistan was a big business and, as I've said, it was easier to kill someone than steal mail.

For some reason I couldn't work out, the company wanted these empty trucks back in Kabul before dark. When Petar told me that the trucks had to be back as soon as possible, I argued that I wouldn't come back during daylight hours. He got Kyle to call me.

'We really need the trucks back,' Kyle said, 'we have visitors tomorrow.' By that he most likely meant US officers from Host-Nation Trucking, coordinators of the mail service on the Afghan side on whom we depended for our military contracts. I would have to get the trucks back and then chaperone Kyle and his buddies when they went out on the town. As military officers, the Host-Nation Trucking guys weren't meant to go off base, it was against all their standing orders—and they certainly weren't meant to be going out drinking and whoring in the Chinese brothels. General order number one dictated no consumption of alcohol or drugs or passage of contraband, including Cuban cigars, among American military personnel. But that's what they would do, because that's how we got the contracts.

All six of our security vehicles were from Mansour's team based in Ghazni. By this time, we had built good trust. I was often out on my own with them, as the only westerner, and I never doubted them. There might have been an element among them that thought, from time to time, *Let's kill the white guy*, but Mansour was in control. I trusted him one hundred per cent. Maybe ninety per cent.

I delayed leaving Ghazni as long as possible, figuring that if I left late in the afternoon I could travel under cover of darkness, which I always preferred, and still get back to the compound before Kyle wanted to go out. As night was falling, we were approaching Salar. It was cool and cloudless, and at that time of year the night closed in quickly.

Tired after three days out with the convoy, moving only at night, I was pissed off at having to rush back. We'd had no contacts, which was good, but the constant work was not good for my head. Our vehicles were marked and we were in touch with the American military. It was a bit stressful when drones came overhead and put their infra-red searchlights on us. Here I was with heavy weapons and a bunch of Afghans, on edge whenever I saw a US drone. I would get on the phone to the Americans, give them a friendly call sign and say, 'Don't light us up, please, we've got your mail!'

I was due a bit of downtime.

At around 5.15pm, as we neared Salar, we were providing what was called 'bounding overwatch', which meant that our vehicles were leapfrogging each other ahead of the convoy, with the lead vehicle stopping to take up a potential firing position while the next one took its place at the head of the line. Salar was a fucking nightmare to go through. It's in one of a series of valleys that link up to Pakistan and run down into the green belt, with plenty of trees and vegetation for cover, and the valley of the Helmand River that connects Kabul with the south of Afghanistan, through which the main roads run. The Taliban used the green belt for cover everywhere in the country, but this was particularly hazardous because it connected with the valleys that got them in and out of their safe zones across the Pakistani border.

Just as the machine gunner from our lead vehicle dismounted, that car started taking heavy PKM fire, mostly tracers, from the green belt to our left. It was pretty nasty and began smashing into the trucks. The two truck drivers legged it towards the buildings to the right-hand side of the road, though I only saw one of them running off and initially didn't realise he was a driver.

The head and tail of our security team became disconnected almost immediately. Both groups of three cars pulled off to the right shoulder and the guys began to return fire, but our two groups were about six hundred metres apart. Mansour was with the trio of cars up front, while I was at the rear. By radio, I was coordinating two call signs that were pinned down in different places. It wasn't ideal.

Mohammed drove our car up next to the trucks, where I intended to get them moving again. But when I saw that the drivers had disappeared, I pulled off down to the right as well and took cover behind a couple of wrecks from previous ambushes (a clear sign that this was a bad area; the insurgents didn't have a whole lot of imagination, and if a previous place had worked for them, they'd go there again and again until they were caught. They did things the same way their fathers did against the Russians, so if you saw old Russian wrecks and newer wrecks, such as those lying by the roadside here, get ready.)

Behind me was a large walled compound, and a line of trees ran from the corner of the wall to the roadside; it was down that line that the drivers had presumably run.

The PKM and AK fire was mainly directed at the trucks and at Mansour's position. From the volume of the gunfire, I estimated that there were probably no more than ten insurgents.

4 Section, 9 Platoon, C Company, 1RAR in Timor Leste, January 2001.

Team Leader with
Edinburgh International
on Operation Artemis,
Baghdad, 2005. Shortly
after the first Iraqi
elections.

Preparing for an airport run along the notorious Route 'Irish' outside
Baghdad's Green Zone, Operation Artemis, 2005.

Near Gardez, Afghanistan, in 2009, with SD (left) and Frank (centre).
On the way to get 'Rosie', the three-year-old girl who had been burnt.
(Photo Marcus Wilson)

Two of the good guys in Afghanistan, medics KC (left) and Marcus (right).

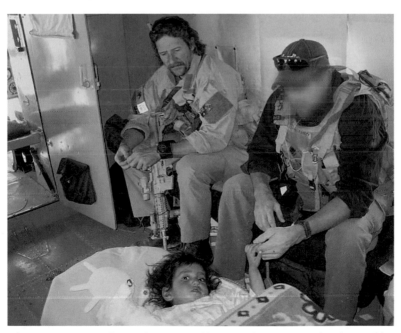

The opportunity to do good came up all too rarely. 'Rosie', a three-year-old girl, had been burnt by her family to get money from the Americans. Marcus, Frank and I helped get her on a helicopter to a proper hospital.
(Photo Credit Marcus Wilson)

Top of the Garden Range, 2009. All the provinces had the gates built on the roads leading in.

Watching a convoy in the 'Green Belt' near Salar—the local word for 'rifle'.

My personal kit. Because the company was not spending money as it was meant to, I had to buy most of it myself.

Pol-e-Charkhi as I never saw it, from the outside. The outside fences were superfluous: as you can see, there was nowhere to run. (Photo Steve Kenny)

In Block 4, the corridor outside the living area was covered in graffiti and burn marks—the aftermath of the earlier riots in 2005, long before I got there.

This is not the aftermath of a riot—it's how the other half lived. One of the Afghan prisoners' living areas in Block 4. (Getty Images/Mario Tama)

Hangings in Pol-e-Charkhi were messy. When the condemned men hung from this gallow, their feet often touched the ground and they strangled slowly. (Getty Images/Wakil Kohsar/AFP)

The nooses. All those chairs are set up for politicians and dignitaries to watch the hangings. (Getty Images/Nur Photo)

The 'gym' where we worked out in the Nigerian–Ugandan living area, Block 4. The equipment was all homemade.

A communal meal with the Africans, Block 4, 2010.

Kettle bells and dumbbells made by pouring stolen cement into empty drink containers.

A day's food for five people: Block 4, 2011.

The western view from Block 4, winter 2011. Even with the thickness of the walls and the small windows, the winter cold was severe.

A makeshift volleyball court, Pol-e-Charkhi. I never saw this. (Getty Images/ Massoud Hossaini)

View to the north, winter 2011. The large tower is a water pressure tank, not a guard tower.

In Block 4, the Africans made home brew by fermenting anything from tomatoes to apricots. Funnily, the master brewer was Abdelrahman, a practising Muslim who didn't drink.

Visiting day, Block 4, 2011. Some of those tents were set up for prisoners to enjoy some intimacy with their visiting wives.

My sleeping space inside Block 4. Not luxurious, but bearable.

A product of my
environment, Block 4,
2012.

The Afghan National Police's own crop: they grew marijuana outside Block 10 and sold it to the prisoners.

The police's weed harvest, Block 10, 2016.

Adelaide lawyer Steve Kenny looked after the Australian end and visited Pol-e-Charkhi in 2011. (Photo Nathan Amy)

Shitty the cat on one of her favourite perches, 2015. I wouldn't be surprised if she's running the prison by now.

The beacon: once Kim Motley got involved with my case, I was headed for freedom. This is on 31 July 2016. I am waiting to sign release papers. An hour earlier, I was in my cell. (Photo Jessica Donati)

Out! Chatting with Kim, 31 July 2016. And a lot of Afghan officials looking for the opportunity to show the world what good people they are. (Photo Greg Pye)

In the days immediately after my release, I stayed in Kabul to decompress—and did some close protection work for Kim. (Photo Joel Van Houdt)

With Kim at Kabul Airport, waiting to leave. The same place I'd been so close to getting out of seven years earlier. (Photo Joel Van Houdt)

Over the next little while, I linked our two groups together near the trucks and talked to Mansour.

'Where are the drivers?' I said through Mohammed.

Mansour didn't know. We had a fair idea that one had run to the compound, but we had no idea about the other. I couldn't call them on my phone. They weren't allowed to carry arms or cell phones: I could never be sure that a driver wasn't telling his Taliban brother—or telling his wife who told her friend who told her Taliban brother-in-law's best mate—where we were and where we were going. It was such a small world, I used to call them a bunch of Esmes, after the old gossip in *A Country Practice*.

But now, as I couldn't trust them to have phones, we couldn't contact them.

I called the Four Horsemen office. Petar and the Macedonians were out to dinner. The signal was also bad, but I eventually got hold of one of the Afghans and told him our grid reference and the current situation. 'Fucking get Junior in there so he can take my next call,' I barked.

Mansour's men were searching for the drivers. The enemy fire had become sporadic, and I was thinking of getting into the trucks ourselves and pulling them off the road, down to the right, where they could be out of harm's way. But every time we tried to get to them, we were hit again. One of Mansour's guys went over to a truck and started it up, and the left side of it got shot up so badly it wasn't going to move again. I would later blow it up with an RPG: another body for that truck graveyard.

Mohammed, our PKM gunner and I moved forward to engage the enemy, leapfrogging each other up the right-hand side of the road: one half moving, the other providing covering fire, standard infantry movement. We were fired on by more AKs, much closer to the trucks than where they'd been initially. They were actually coming after us, not just disabling our trucks and running away.

Bam. They didn't just have AKs and machine guns. They fired two RPGs, which sailed harmlessly over our heads. I also carried an RPG for each vehicle. It's an awesome weapon, not so effective on armoured vehicles, but very much so on lighter vehicles, some buildings and people in the open. The different types of rocket available vary from place to place but the familiar PG (high explosive) and BG (anti-personnel) are the most common.

But not always foolproof. One of our guys loaded up an RPG and fired back. He was putting in another round when one of his Afghan mates ran over to talk to him. He didn't realise the first guy was about to fire, and the noise and sound wave of the back blast blew the second guy's eardrums out. All of a sudden he began yelling; he couldn't hear anything. Then the gunner was yelling back. Then other yellers joined in. It turned into a bit of a comedy. They were arguing, and I began yelling too: 'Just shut up and keep shooting!'

We took the deafened guy to his vehicle and left him there with Mohammed and another bloke. I went back towards Mansour, who was trying to organise his remaining men. We joined up together and got into another stoush. We cleaned up the insurgent, and I picked up his RPG. That was mine now.

I was coming to realise that my initial estimate of ten enemy was conservative. We got up to the non-disabled truck and were shot to fuck, first by AKs and then by RPGs. They fired one RPG round that bounced off the road, smacked into a wall of the compound and exploded. The rounds self-detonate at one kilometre after being fired. Some

Afghans were able to judge the distance so well, they could shoot for distance rather than at a target. An RPG round will self-detonate at about 900 metres, so the Afghans would try to get that to happen over the top of people behind cover. They could be clever bastards.

Having been hammered when we got near our trucks, we pulled back towards the wrecks, covering ourselves with fire towards the insurgents. Their returning fire began to peter out a little bit, coming from further away and going over our heads.

I got on the phone to the office. They said Petar was still at dinner. Junior hadn't been called in. I was furious.

'Don't the Americans know we're in a contact?' I screamed. We needed military support of some description. Otherwise we might well be toast.

'No.'

So I rang Junior myself. He understood the situation instantly and went straight back to the office, basically taking over at their end. He rang the guys at FOB Airborne and let them know friendlies—an expat with a convoy—were in contact. If he'd told them I was Australian, they might not have done anything to help. But it was an American convoy and he was an American and, clever kid, he phrased things exactly the right way.

Although the intensity of the assault had dropped off, every time we moved back towards the wrecks we got hit again.

'So what are you doing now, man?' Junior said.

'Lying on my back watching tracers flying over my fucking face.'

I was seriously considering putting my helmet on.

While I was on the phone, Mansour turned up and said, 'I've found a body.'

'Who?'

'I don't know. He's got no head.'

Because Mansour did not speak English, every communication between us had to be interpreted by Mohammed. My terp and driver was translating, fighting, and working shit out for me while I was both giving Junior information on the phone and trying to understand what Mansour was saying. Mohammed was an awesome kid. He crept to our car and got a body bag out. We bagged the dead guy and put him into one of Mansour's cars.

There was a bit of a lull as we sorted out our ammunition, getting more from the car. We also took the magazines off any of the enemy that we cleaned up. That was the beauty of using AKs, the same weapon as them.

Meanwhile, FOB Airborne, fifty kilometres away, were trying to put together a QRF: a Quick Reaction Force. But they were having trouble doing it quickly enough for us. They had a team at that FOB but it was out on an operation. That was a shame, because they would have been very handy at this point.

Mansour and I discussed who the headless guy might be. I thought it could be one of our drivers. That made sense. But I had too much on my plate to try to piece it all together, and Mansour and his crew absolutely did not give a shit. We would figure that out later.

Amazingly, while all of this was going on, there was road traffic coming through from Ghazni, to our south. This was not unusual during an ambush, believe it or not. Afghan drivers would stop while the bullets and RPGs were flying about, but inevitably they would get impatient and try to drive through it. This one dude in a taxi drove up into the middle of the fight, parked right between us and the insurgents, and tried to get us to stop shooting so he could get his fare! His headlights were on us, illuminating us for the insurgents' benefit, whether intentionally or not. I was thinking, *Are you fucking serious?* So we shot the lights out of his car. That made him get out of the way.

But because of the taxi driver's actions, the enemy knew where we were and we got creamed. Four or five of them came at us with AKs and PKMs. We moved around so we wouldn't get shot at so much. Whenever we stopped, they assumed they had nailed us. The group who were coming in our direction moved along the wall of the compound towards us, but when they came into the open the tables were turned: we could see them in silhouette, lit up by the stationary traffic. We put an RPG round into them, finishing off the first guys. One of Mansour's dudes with a PKM cleaned up those who couldn't run away.

People then began firing at us from the line of trees behind. We held where we were. We didn't even know if they were ours or theirs—they were just Afghans carrying guns. So we shot them. Fortunately, they were enemy. But it was so chaotic, we were more or less firing on suspicion at anyone with a gun.

Junior rang me up, and said the guys at FOB Airborne were going to come in with a full fire mission, using 120mm mortar rounds. It's a very serious business when the Americans come in with fire support, and you can't afford to make mistakes calling them in. I would be guiding their fire by speaking to Junior on the phone and him relaying it to the mortar line. Too much could go wrong; you're supposed to have direct communication between the ground and the tubes.

I said to Junior, 'Can they put up illum rounds?'

Illumination rounds float above you on parachutes and light everything up. They have a range of up to seven kilometres and will illuminate a one-kilometre square for forty or fifty seconds. I had Night Vision Goggles, but the illumination would help my guys see the bad guys. Even if we didn't have indirect fire support, the illumination would work in our favour. Junior said he would see what he could do.

Mohammed took our vehicle closer to Mansour, with the rest of us covering him and then following on foot so that we had now consolidated. We took cover in a culvert. Through Mohammed, I said to our guys, 'Stay down when the illum rounds go up, but fire on anyone who's on the road or on the other side.'

With the illum rounds up, I had our guys lie down as still as statues. We let the insurgents move, and then we smacked them.

There was a bunch of dudes trying to get into our second truck, the less shot-up one. We shot them. Then we saw a bunch further down, near the wrecks, shooting from a culvert under the road. I said to Mohammed, 'Ask Mansour if they're ours or theirs.' He said, 'They're not ours.'

We got into an extended line and walked down, paralleling the road. They didn't even see us coming. When we were right on top of them, no more than twenty metres away, one let off a burst from his machine gun into the culvert. One of my guys got a fright, and shot a round straight into the dirt. Having lost the element of surprise at the last moment, we opened up.

While I was firing, I ran out of ammo. I hadn't checked my mag. *Bang bang bang . . . click!* I don't think I had ever experienced true stress in battle until this point. I'd even taught the subject to diggers in Australia, but had never gone through it myself. Time really did slow down and I got tunnel vision. It was strange. But what helped was that because I'd been taught to expect it, and had studied it at length, it didn't freak me out. I tried to go with the slowness of time and use it to get things done. I pulled out my pistol and fired a whole seventeen-shot mag at one of the insurgents. We dropped all five of them.

All of a sudden, a pained screaming came out of the dark a few steps away. We looked into the culvert where they'd been firing from and saw a man lying there, clutching his leg, which had been shot off below the knee. It was virtually hanging off by a bit of skin. He had taken a few rounds in his stomach as well. He was one of our drivers, the one I already knew from earlier jobs. He had been hiding in this culvert, and the enemy had been dragging him out when we came upon them.

I patched him up as best I could. His leg was flopping around, so I applied a tourniquet to his stump and got him onto an improvised stretcher (an Afghan scarf) to lift him onto one of our cars.

Another of our team, who had been close to me on my right, had been shot through the arm. The round tore out a chunk of flesh. I dressed it and tied him up, and he was ready to go.

A lull followed, and I took the opportunity to check out our trucks. The one the enemy had got to was shot up badly and was in flames. We couldn't take it. The other one was badly damaged too, so I punched an RPG round into it, blowing it up. We didn't want to leave anything for them.

It was time to get out. I got hold of Junior on the sat phone. The Americans had been holding off on CAirS, or full-on air support, until we were out of the area.

'Mate, we're getting out of here now,' I said. 'Whatever the Americans can do would be nice. Like right now. See you when I see you.'

I gave one of my strobes to Mansour and told him to tape it to the roof of his car. I already had one on my helmet. They would go off in the dark, and clearly show the Americans—we hoped—that we were friendly and not targets.

With our headlights switched off, we pulled onto the shoulder of the road and sped off along the berm. We must have hit every single culvert; our RPGs were smashing up and down with every bump. The transmission diff on our car cracked, and, as soon as we could, we pulled up onto the paved road, whacked on our headlights, and went for broke, the engine making all sorts of weird clanking noises. Behind us, all we could hear was big guns firing from above and shells exploding. I don't know if the Americans sent in A-10 Warthogs or a Spectre, the Hercules gunship that is like the hand of God. I just hoped like hell we were far enough away. When we got to Maidan Shar, we pulled into the petrol station and took stock of our situation. We had the two wounded—the driver with his leg shot off and the security guy with the injured arm. Another of the team had been hit in the chest by a round that had bounced off the road, but he wasn't hurt. Some guys had small frag injuries. It was pretty surprising, and fortunate that we came out of it with only one fatality, the headless guy, who we assumed was the second truck driver.

One of Four Horsemen's other security teams, who were quartered closer to Kabul in a town called Logar, were waiting for us at Maidan Shar. They were supposed to have come and helped us, but said, 'Oh, we didn't have any fuel.' Yeah, right. They were Panjshiris. My Pashtun guys were ready to kill them. 'You fucking bunch of dogs,' Mansour muttered. It got really heated, as it does when you've been fighting for four hours.

Their failure to join us was another example of Commander Haussedin's treachery. In charge of that other team was a guy called Engineer, who'd worked for Hausseddin ever since their Northern Alliance days during the Russian occupation. It turned out that they had been listening to the whole thing going off. They had enough fuel to drive two hours back to where they came from, so I assume that the only reason they didn't come and help us was that they were gutless or they wanted us to get smashed.

If there was ever a chance they'd get hurt, these groups took a day off. They held the company to ransom. If we didn't employ them, they would turn against us. Even when we did employ them, they were too cowardly to join any serious fight. They were instinctive saboteurs. On one occasion, Engineer had said we couldn't use his vehicles, so Mohammed sorted out some replacements. Within two days, all the fuel tanks had been sugared and the tyres had been let down. The NDS sprang a surprise visit and demanded to see our weapons licences. When I handed them over, the NDS agents were reading the licences upside down. They couldn't even read. It was a joke. The message was that we needed to pay Haussedin's people protection money, or else.

But I didn't want Engineer's and Mansour's groups to start shooting at each other, after all we'd been through that night, so I told Engineer and his men to piss off. We were only two kilometres from FOB Airborne, where the medics had been prepped for our wounded security guys, and we had to get the driver with the blown-off leg to the hospital in the town of Maidan Shar. That turned out to be a waste of time, as the hospital was not equipped to deal with that kind of injury, so the US military told us to take him to the base, which was a couple of kilometres to the west of the town. Not so simple.

It was dark and we hadn't been there before, our cars had had their lights shot out, and we couldn't find the FOB. As we were driving around, we came across an injured civilian Afghan who walked up to us and flagged us down. I was pretty sure he was one of the dudes who'd lit us up. He was begging us to take him to the town hospital. I said, 'We'll take you to the Americans, they'll fix you up.' He decided he didn't want to come anymore.

As we drove around looking, we were hitting every pothole while I was in the back tray trying to keep the injured truck driver happy. Eventually, out of nowhere, this guy in an American uniform appeared: no body armour, just a pistol and a flashlight.

'Dude,' I said, 'what are you doing out here on your own?'

'I've come out to meet you guys and let you in because I figured you hadn't been here before.'

'You'd better not let your CO know about this,' I said.

'The CO's okay,' he smiled, 'but I might get in trouble with my top sergeant.' Then he introduced himself: he was Captain Hill, the CO of the base. Fucking gutsy. He'd just cruised out by himself. 'I wouldn't risk my men to do this, so I did it myself,' he said. I liked this guy.

I sat with Captain Hill's top sergeant while the doctors sorted out our guys. The one who had been deafened by the RPG blast had a perforated eardrum, and the guy with the bullet in his arm had a messy wound but no complications. Unfortunately the driver was likely to lose his leg, and he and the bloke with the arm wound were to be flown out to the big US military hospital at Bagram.

Mansour and his uninjured team members camped outside overnight, while I tried to get them some more ammunition that had been captured from the insurgency and kept at the FOB. I debriefed the key American personnel, including Captain Hill and his top sergeant.

(An interesting but sad footnote: Captain Hill and his top sergeant were later dishonourably discharged from the US Army after an incident when they had discovered that some of their interpreters were feeding information to the Taliban in the Salar area. To find out which were guilty, they put the terps in a room and said, 'Righteo guys, here's what we're going to do. We're going to ask who's giving information to the Taliban, one at a time. Who's first?' They asked a guy, and he said no. They took him outside, away from the others, and fired a single pistol round into the side of the building. Everyone inside heard it, and thought the terp had been shot. Then Hill and his sergeant came back in and said, 'Who's next?' They eventually found out who it was. It was important because they were losing guys every month; their patrols were getting cleaned up outside the wire. I'd have done the same thing in his shoes, and he saved the lives of his men. He also did a favour to the terps, who would have all been sent to Guantanamo and been water-boarded if Captain Hill had followed the manual. All he had done was scare them. He was a terrific bloke and really could have gone a long way. His discharge was a sad thing to hear about. The good guys weren't allowed to bend the rules, apparently.)

After getting a feed, Mohammed and I fucked off back to Kabul on our own. On the way, our cracked diff finally gave out and we were leaking oil. The car died when we were on the outskirts of Kabul, near a market. Four Horsemen sent us another vehicle, and we only got a kilometre out of it before it ran out of fuel—they hadn't bothered to fill it up. By then I wasn't in a great mood.

When we got back, Kyle was at the compound with his mate from Host-Nation Trucking, a captain in the US Army. Kyle was complaining because he had wanted to go out on the town and now it was too late.

I said, 'I've been in a firefight for four hours and you're hooking into me? You can go fuck yourselves.'

The officer told me I couldn't talk to him like that. 'I'm a captain!'

'No,' I said calmly, 'I'm a civilian, I can talk to you any way I want. Fuck off, I'm going to write my report.'

I wrote my report, cleaned my kit while I had three beers, and that was me gone. Next day I woke up and got ready to go again. Keep going. You learn to defuse it. You clean your weapons, prepare your magazines, clean your clothing and other gear. The tasks help you wind down.

There remained some fallout. Remember the second truck driver who disappeared, who I thought must have been the headless body? The next day, that second truck driver turned up at our compound—in a taxi. So fuck knows who the headless body was. I never confirmed it.

The driver who'd had his leg shot up? Two weeks later, he showed up at the Four Horsemen compound. All he wanted was to shake my hand to thank me for bringing him back to his family. I thought, *There, I've done some good.* John Allen gave him several grand out of his own pocket. He didn't have to do that. The way he saw it, this guy had lost his leg supporting the US military, so he deserved something. I respected acts like that. Kyle was carrying on about the payment because he thought it came out of company funds. John let him go on and then said, 'I paid for that out of my own pocket.'

Kyle said, 'Oh. But you shouldn't be giving it to Afghans.'

John said, 'You're missing the point. This is why we're here.'

Kyle personified all the problems in fighting war for profit. John personified some—*some*—of the virtues.

For myself, that night set in stone the relationship I had with my Afghan crew. My guys knew I would do anything for them. I would not run away, I would go back into a firefight and get them out. 'The foreigner with the painted arms,' they said, 'he'll come back for you.'

But the whole incident raised questions for me. My team and I had been put at risk for what? After I returned to the compound, the trucks that we had risked our lives to try to bring back were never mentioned.

8

Dead man walking

The third time I received the death sentence, I wasn't even at the hearing. There was no spoken evidence, just a handing-down of the judgment by the court. No one told me it was happening, and there was no input from any lawyers. It was a farce from the start. To be honest, I'd have had more respect for their system if they just went ahead and hanged me. I wouldn't have enjoyed it too much, but at least it wouldn't have been ridiculous.

For my lawyer Bashir and his intermediaries, the whole process was one big money-making scheme. Through a guy called Karim, who acted as a fixer for Scotty and Dave, Bashir kept asking for more. There was an Afghan business-man who was apparently going to secure my release through his political connections. It was more bullshit. Every step of the way, I believed they were conning my sister out of more money. There was always one last bribe, and then another last bribe, and Rob would be free. It ended up leading to friction between Katie and me. We would have phone calls where I'd be saying, 'Don't give them anything,' and she would reply, 'But he said that if we paid this much to this guy . . .'

I told her to stop. 'They're lying to you,' I said. But she was desperate: 'No, they're saying it will get you out!' The irony in this was that Katie was actually refusing every suggestion that she pay bribes, despite a lot of pressure. Glen asked her for US$25,000 once, and then later he called her to say he had a boat in Queensland, and if she would buy it from him for US$100,000, he would use the proceeds to get me out. Katie flat-out refused. To give her credit, she ran every money question past me and called me to check out every new person who contacted her in connection with me. She was totally solid. The problem was, my mental state was so precarious, I would imagine all kinds of people pressuring her to give them money, and her not being able to resist. I should have trusted her more, but my inability to do so is just another sign of that mental disarray.

In that first year, my imprisonment and the death sentences were placing my family under unbelievable strain. After two months of dealing with everything through Katie, I finally spoke to my parents, and it wasn't easy. They didn't know what to say to me. There was no process, no certainty, just a vague likelihood of a death penalty but more probably a very long prison term, maybe for the rest of my life. Almost certainly, I would be in there for the rest of Mum and Dad's lives. I was sure the anxiety was doing their heads in, and we found it difficult even to get to first base of a rational conversation. I didn't want them or Katie coming over; it was too dangerous and could be too traumatising for them.

I withdrew into myself again, hoping in a way that my family could get on with their lives and not be thinking about me, assuring them that I would survive day by day in my little shell.

In the end, not even Bashir turned up to my third hearing. It was the police in prison who told me I'd been given the death sentence again. I had one question: 'Did my lawyer turn up?'

My third death sentence came two or three months after the previous hearing. By then I had been moved permanently to Pol-e-Charkhi, which made it difficult to get any embassy help, due to their difficulties travelling from Kabul. Ivan kept turning up with supplies and documents from the embassy, even when the diplomats had been told not to come.

Scotty and Dave were my most constant link with the outside. They brought in boxes of twelve MREs (Meals Ready to Eat, or US Army ration packs). Some of them were okay and some were absolute crap. At least they had plenty in them. One meal was the size of an Australian 24-hour ration pack—that's how big the American rations were, and I began to put on weight. It was an interesting mix of food. Along with burritos, meat and vegetables, there were heaps of sweets: M&Ms, Reese's Pieces, pound cakes, biscuits and chocolate brownies. The Afghan prisoners would say, 'Give us some American food.' When I had to make my own entertainment or if I was in a malicious mood, I would give them some pork and watch their reactions.

———

Once I was in Pol-e-Charkhi, the reality of the death penalty sank in. Executions were carried out by hanging, and an

A-frame steel structure, like a swing set, was erected in the visitors' yard. There was no notice. Before my time, the authorities had had a problem with executions. They would tell a prisoner he was going to be hanged. Then he'd contact the Red Cross, who would set in motion an appeal with the Afghan government. So now they did it without notice. Every few months, the guards would go through the cells and round up the condemned men. Muslims don't approve of the American way of having capital offenders stuck on death row for year after year. They believe it's more merciful to get on with the job. So they do.

The guards would drag out twenty guys per session, tie them one at a time by the neck to the horizontal bar of the swing set, stand them on plastic chairs, and then kick the chair away. It was that primitive. It's a horrible way to die, a slow and noisy strangulation rather than the swift drop you imagine. After killing each other for thousands of years, they should be better at it, but they were shithouse. I went out once, stood under the swing set and put my hands up. My wrists touched the bar. If it happened to me, I would take ages to die, half-suspended between the bar and the ground. After that, and having seen a few executions, I said to a guard who spoke some English, 'If my turn comes, can you guys please shoot me instead?'

It's hard to remember and describe my personal feeling of 'I am going to die here'. Until my first sentencing, it didn't cross my mind. After I was condemned, I refused to believe it. When the second and third sentences were handed down, I actually reacted with scepticism and indifference, firstly because I thought I was more likely to die from foul play and secondly because I began to sense that if they hadn't executed me already, there was a growing possibility that they weren't going to. But those were my brighter, more lucid moments.

In between were waves of bleak and dark thoughts, which sometimes accumulated into a wall of depression. I was going to die here. Not from hanging, though. Not from foul play. I was going to kill myself. I would call up poor Katie and say, 'I'm going to do myself in.' I would rant and rave about all the people and the things I hated and how I couldn't take this place anymore. Katie would stay silent, terrified of saying the wrong thing, a chance word that might set me off. She just listened and kept her input calm and practical. I really did want to kill myself during these periods. But the feeling would lift, and I called Katie back and said, 'I'm sorry, but you're the only person I've got that I can say this stuff to.' She understood this, fortunately. I just needed to hear myself say it—*I am going to end myself*—before I could shake myself up and break free of it.

During that first year and a half, until Scotty and Dave got hold of MREs to send in, my body was showing the signs of this losing battle. The food I had got from embassy visits at Tolkeef was never enough after I shared it around, and I lost a lot of weight. I stand 186 centimetres tall and weighed around 92 or 93 kilos before I went in. During that first year or so, I shed about 15 kilograms. I was doing little or no exercise, as my days and nights in Tolkeef were spent curled on my bed, the only space that I had even a modicum of privacy in. I was gaunt and weak and constantly stressed. Looking back, probably the beginning of my mental recovery was Dave and Scotty bringing those MREs. Once I was getting a bit more nutrition into me, I could think clearly and begin to set out a daily survival plan. But this took a long period of adjustment. You need to stop believing you're going to be freed any day before you start to adjust to prison life as your reality, and it was not until I had been at Pol-e-Charkhi for some months before I began to think, *This is where I live now*. And that in itself was not an easy thing to accept.

9

Little Africa

When I arrived at Pol-e-Charkhi for the final time, after the hot water incident, I was placed in Block 4. In many ways, this move saved my life.

There were periodic riots in the jail, when large masses of Afghan prisoners would set anything flammable, such as bedding and clothes, on fire and try to destroy the place. During the most recent one, the foreign prisoners were all moved to the top floor of Block 4. This is where I was assigned. Most of the foreigners were Africans—Nigerian and Ugandan drug traffickers and mules—and when they were moved into this part of Block 4, they cleaned it up so well that the Afghans wanted to move back in.

Where my previous experience in Tolkeef was all about hostility and being on guard, the top floor of Block 4 was much more open and relaxed. The Nigerian and Ugandan prisoners had that whole floor to themselves. It was a large overall area, about the size of a quarter of a football field. The concrete walls were still blackened by soot from a previous fire. The middle of the concrete area was made up of a single large cage with a hallway, about three metres wide, running around it. Little tents made up of Red Cross blankets, Afghan carpets and sheets of plastic were set up inside the cage area, and clothes were hanging everywhere on the bars. Some of the floor space was taken up with cooking utensils and boxes of food, pushed against the walls or the cage so that you wouldn't trip over them. There were windows set into the concrete side walls, and you could climb up and see the other blocks and the sandy courtyards between each 'spoke' of the prison, as well as the high tube-shaped water tower. During the infamous 2008 riots, before I arrived at Pol-e-Charkhi, the army had set up a PKM on the water tower and randomly fired into the blocks below. You could still see the bullet holes and marks in the walls of Block 4.

The predominant smell was of cooking, which took place in a communal area beside the cage. Once a week the Africans did big one-pot soups and stews, ladled out of large aluminium saucepans to feed the whole group. The Africans stacked up some homemade weights and other exercise equipment they had improvised, and in their tents they kept phones and even TVs and DVD players. Compared with where I had been, it was civilised, clean and—well, not luxurious, but these things are all relative.

I had met most of them at Tolkeef, including their leaders, Ken and Abdelrahman. As with most of the Africans, they hung out in shorts and thongs. I liked them and was relieved to be with them in Block 4 rather than the hell of Block 7 or the limbo of Tolkeef. I ended up staying there for nearly two years. It was just one floor but it made all the difference. I was lucky that there were some good officers in the prison system: it had been the 2IC of Tolkeef who sent the order across that I be sent upstairs.

There were up to eighteen Africans on that floor at different times, mostly on drug-smuggling convictions. Six younger ones had turned up at Tolkeef around the same time as me. The young guys were just couriers, paying off student loans or saving up to buy a house or start a business. They wanted to do one run and get ahead, but they'd drawn the wrong number in the smugglers' lottery. Even though they tended to get arrested at the airport in groups, they got all sorts of separate sentences. Three of them—Derek, Zumi and Iqra— had been arrested together, but Derek got eighteen years, Zumi ten and Iqra six. Go figure. Maybe to balance things out, they were all released more or less together, in 2016.

The head of the Nigerians was Paul Chigga, who was in Pol-e-Charkhi for nine years, seven of them before I arrived. Midnight-black with long dreadlocks, he spoke perfect Dari (of which he taught me a few useful words and phrases), he trained every day, and he had his shit together. There was also a Ugandan, Iqra, who got around with a withered arm thanks to a childhood attack of polio, and was studying to be a mullah. Everyone was doing whatever it took to get them through.

I was closest to Ken and Abdelrahman, who were not mules but professional smugglers. It was their job and they knew the risks. I respected that they were honest about it and didn't do their job half-baked. As they explained it to me, on any drug run, there were several other people you didn't know. On a good day you all got through, and on a bad day a random number of you would get picked up. You might have been arrested in the same group, but you didn't end up getting to know each other until you were in jail.

Being with the Nigerians was the first time that I began to settle down a little. With the MRE boxes, which were made from cardboard tough enough to throw out of helicopters, we covered the windows and built partitions for separate sleeping areas, and I was taken into the fold of a civilised community. Food was a strong source of connection. The Africans gave me fresh vegies, which were not part of the standard MREs, and in return I asked Dave and Scotty to bring in foods the Africans wanted if they could find them in Kabul, such as okra and sugi, a dumpling the Africans made from bread dough and ate like a damper.

I put on some beef by training like an animal with home-made weights. There was always building work going on at the jail and Paul Chigga had conned some powdered concrete out of the builders. We mixed it with dirt and gravel from the exercise yard and set the concrete inside oil containers that we managed to get from the prison kitchen. We used a pipe we ripped out of the non-functioning plumbing system as the cross bar. With a Russian prisoner called Andre, I filled up some long two-litre plastic water bottles with the mixture and when they set, these were our kettle bells. Every day I woke up with a plan for what weights exercises I was going to do. I never left the floor we were on, so all of my work was indoors. But I went hard at the improvised weights, and with the better food from my MREs and the vegetables the Africans had, I eventually began to get back to my normal physique. By the end of the time I spent with them in Block 4, I was a beast: 90 kilos plus of solid muscle. It was a physical expression of how my mind was recovering from the worst of the depression. The down times had not finished, don't worry about that, but the waves began to get spaced further and further apart.

I never really left the Africans' area unless I had to. I didn't like going through the 'zoo', as we called it, where the Afghans were. Sometimes a prisoner would have a crack at me and when I got really big I could hurt them, but that only risked being sent back for some re-education in Block 7. So I tried to stay on the Nigerians' floor twenty-four hours a day, unless the embassy or Scotty and Dave came to meet me in the visiting area.

For those first months, I wasn't up with the who's-who-in-the-zoo divisions of the prisoner population. It was just me against the world. The one group that was conspicuous was the Taliban, who at that stage were scattered through the jail among other criminals, a lot of whom were drug traffickers and would-be gangsters, who were probably not as serious in the criminal world as even Australian gangsters. But the Taliban were definitely serious. They were among the general population because they paid bribes to get their terrorism charges changed to drug or violence charges. Then they could negotiate reductions in their terms, which were not possible under terrorism charges. They knew every trick.

They were different. These were not even top-end Taliban, who were held at a nearby military prison and, for the very top ones, at the black US prison at the Bagram air base. (But even there, they managed to smuggle in phones and cameras. Later, when I met the Taliban mufti Hakemi and he talked to those guys on their phones, I asked how the Taliban leaders got their cameras and phones into Bagram, hinting that they secreted them up their arses. Hakemi said, 'This is a thing we don't talk about!') One thing that was most conspicuous about the Taliban prisoners was their organisation. They were clean, they dressed immaculately and they wore the Taliban's distinctive black scarf. They had a hygiene and discipline that you didn't see with other Afghans. They got together as a group and practised martial arts. They were not visibly scared of anything. Other prisoners and even guards automatically deferred to them, and they would come into fights to settle them down or order prisoners to clean up their cells. Always, they were obeyed. One of the few times I saw the Taliban lose their cool was at a hanging. Unlike most other capital offenders, who wept and pleaded for mercy, the Taliban would march to the gallows with their heads high, and die silently. But on one occasion, the guards hanged them without acknowledging them as political prisoners, just announcing each one as a rapist or a murderer. With their 'freedom fighter' status taken from them, the Taliban guys got very angry and upset. It only happened that once. Otherwise, the prison authorities were content to let the Taliban prisoners run their own race and keep order their own way. It was probably a microcosm of how the whole country was running under President Karzai.

Outside of the relative peace of the top floor, it wasn't that I went out of my way to be a prick to people. It was more an image I wanted to project for my own safety. I gave them fair warning. Why would you mess with a crazy arsehole like me? There were plenty of tough-guy Afghans who thought they were big swinging dicks who frightened westerners. I projected complete fearlessness. What difference would it make to me? I already had a death sentence.

My attitude to the Nigerians and Ugandans was that I could talk to them and live among them but not fully trust them. Abdelrahman, maybe, was the one exception. He was a genuinely good guy, who even organised to send gifts such as beaded necklaces to my little niece Maddie in South Australia. The Afghan guards gave Abdelrahman a hard time for not being a real Muslim—apparently because he was black—but to prove his credentials he got his uncle, the local mufti in his village in Nigeria, on the phone to speak Arabic to them. It gave him instant credibility and freaked them right out. He was a good bloke and I could talk to him about whatever troubles I had.

Those troubles seemed to stem from the fact that as a group the Africans were addicted to gossip and talking about each other behind their backs, creating tension and politics that I thought were unnecessary. Boredom in prison is the major cause of tension, and the Nigerians and Ugandans, when they got bored, played mind games. One of them, Richard, thought he was the master at playing the other Africans off against each other. He was one of the guys who was always jockeying to be top dog. He would sidle up to me and say, 'So-and-so said bad things about you . . . what are you gonna do about it?' I tried not to allow myself to be dragged into it, but it was pretty relentless with that group.

'Awesome,' I would reply, to fob him off.

Richard was as camp as they come but very much in the closet, which was understandable given the conservative nature of most of the other Africans. He would give me this intrigued look and say, 'Really? Aren't you angry?'

I would reply, 'I hardly know the bloke. I don't care what he says about me.'

A lot of the time they were trying to wind me up and use me as an attack dog against someone else. If Richard was having an argument with another African, he would try to get me pissed off at the other guy so I would go and beat him up.

The one Nigerian I really did dislike was Abdullah, who would come and pray right near where my head was against the wall of my tent just to rile me. In a highly communal group, he had been forced to sleep alone in one of the few concrete rooms because the other Africans hated him. A dead ringer for Danny Glover but with a Mike Tyson body, Abdullah was as dumb as dogshit. Before prison, he had been offered a job on a smuggling run for some big-time criminals in Nigeria. His job was to go to India, change money for gold, and then spend it on opium which he was to transport back to Nigeria. Instead, he got on the piss in India, spent the money, and had to go home and pay the money back. He blamed some gang member for the initial problem—with Abdullah, everything was somebody else's fault—and he planned to do another drug run to Asia, to get the money to buy a gun, so that he could go back to Nigeria and kill that guy. On his way to the second drug run, he stopped in Dubai and made the same mistake, spending all the syndicate's money on good living. Desperate now, he hooked up with another group of Nigerians to come to Afghanistan to pull off a deal to get money to cover what he'd lost in Dubai. It became a cycle. He set up an arrangement to borrow money from this other group to buy opium in Afghanistan and pay them back later, all with the aim of repaying the guy he had ripped off in the first place. It did your head in just hearing about it. Anyway, he'd been caught by the NDS and here he was.

Abdullah converted to Islam in Pol-e-Charkhi . . . three times. When you converted, the government gave you shoes and clothes and a small amount of money as an enticement. Abdullah did it again and again and kept getting away with it, all for the free shit!

He was not a pleasant person to be around, and the other Nigerians told me to keep my distance. But it was impossible in such a small space, and eventually the volcano blew.

Periodically, the Afghan guards would conduct prison-wide searches for phones and drugs. Because the Africans and I were locked up in a separate area from everyone else, some Afghan prisoners would ask if they could hide their phones among us. I refused, but Abdullah was always open to an opportunity to make some money, so he charged those prisoners to look after their phones during the next search. When the other Nigerians found out what he was doing, one of them hated him enough to tip off the cops.

The cops came to our floor and went straight to Abdullah.

'Where have you hidden the phones?' they said.

'I don't have any phones!' Abdullah pleaded. 'I wouldn't do anything wrong, I wouldn't let my African brothers down!'

The cops said, 'Okay,' and went straight to a bag of Abdullah's clothes that contained about seventeen phones.

'I don't know how they got there!' he cried.

Later, he blamed me for the discovery of the phones. I did have a phone of my own, but I had a number of secret hiding places all around the block in case of searches. My best hiding place was behind the picture of a hot girl in a bikini that I'd taken out of a surf mag someone had sent me. I stuck it on the wall of my tent with a pocket sewn in the blanket behind it. The guards would search everywhere else, but when they saw the girl in her bikini it brought them to a standstill. They'd stare and exclaim how beautiful she was, but never think of looking behind it.

Because I was the outsider, I was an easy target, and Abdullah went on and on about how his getting caught was all my fault. Ken and Abdelrahman were telling him to settle down. But Abdullah simmered away, and a few days later, he was stupid enough to push me when I was cooking my food.

'You're not a Muslim!' he shouted. 'You're not African! You shouldn't be in here.'

'Yeah,' I said, 'but I've been waiting patiently for my turn in the line and I'm cooking now.'

He pushed me again. I slipped behind him and was able to put him in a sleeper hold with my arms around his head and throat. Within seconds he was unconscious and I dropped him on his face on the concrete floor, to add injury to insult.

Paul Chigga, who had the status of boss because he'd been there for the longest, bent down to Abdullah's unconscious body.

'You've killed him,' Paul laughed.

'Nah, he'll wake up.'

Sure enough, Abdullah woke within minutes. He got up and ran off crying to the cops. To get their sympathy, he told them that I'd stopped him praying and I'd beaten him up because he was a Muslim. I was dragged down to the office and asked about the incident. I told them the truth and asked them to question the other Nigerians as witnesses. Paul Chigga came down and said, 'Abdullah's lying, none of that happened.' He told them exactly what had happened and the cops backed off.

From then on, Abdullah held a massive grudge against me. I remember three more times we had scuffles. Although he was huge and muscly, he was not a strong fighter and I managed to knock him down every time. He would go off and mutter and stew, but he couldn't find any support among the others. It was hard to keep the peace when we were in the same room. Everything that went on, he said it was my fault.

His complaints about me sometimes didn't end up the way he planned. Once, he had me sent to the commandant's office for apparently stopping him from praying (I hadn't). The guards brought in a Taliban guy to act as interpreter when they questioned me. He asked where I was from.

'Australia,' I said.

'Australia? I love Australian cricketers!'

Among the books that had been brought in for me, I had one about Shane Warne.

'Shane Warne!' he said. 'You have a book about Shane Warne?'

'Sure,' I said, and arranged to get him the autobiography of the famous Australian cricketer. 'You want to borrow it?'

He was stoked, and the interrogation dwindled away as we chatted about cricket. Abdullah's plan to have me punished was long forgotten.

I had made an enemy in Abdullah, but none of the other Africans would stand up for him. Chigga said, 'Don't worry, when Abdullah goes back to Nigeria, he's dead. He took money from big men.'

'Is he really that stupid?' I said.

'Yeah, he is.'

Another reason some of the Nigerians got a bit unhinged from time to time was that they smoked a lot of hash. Heroin use was rife among the Afghan prisoners and the cops. The guards would smoke hash and opium constantly, and later I discovered they were actually growing marijuana in a plot inside the prison and selling it to the prisoners. Some of the cops were off their heads most of the time. One of the commandants had his office door open and in broad daylight I saw him smoking opium off foil as I walked past after visiting the main office. You could smell the opium smoke wafting down from the cops who were on duty in the guard towers. It affected people differently. Some would behave erratically, while others got sleepy. There was one guard who kept coming to me, stoned off his nut, and asking: 'Anything to eat?'

'No, fuck off.'

'But I'm hungry!'

'Fuck off.'

Throughout my time in the prison, although you couldn't get any medical assistance, if you wanted illegal drugs, you could get anything you wanted, cheaply. You only had to talk to the cops. I steered clear of drugs and didn't do any. There were a lot of reasons for that. Personally, I'd tried almost everything when I went on a bender in South Africa after breaking up with my girlfriend back in late 2007. Drug-taking didn't suit my constitution. I didn't get euphoric or mellow like I was meant to. My brain kept working normally and I found the drug experience pointless. Boring. Then, since I'd been in Afghanistan, I only saw the negative side of what drugs did. There was Haussedin smoking opium all the time and shooting at people without any cause, acting totally mad under the influence. I didn't want to dull my focus. I was on permanent high-alert and had to keep my head clear. I could see that once you set foot on that slippery slope in jail, there was no coming back.

I always loved a drink, though, and I took the opportunity to drink the palm wine and potato vodka that the Nigerians and other prisoners were able to make. We had a nice Christmas in 2010. We made a still out of pipes, plastic buckets and other bits and pieces we cobbled together, and fermented tomatoes. For every couple of litres of liquid, we got a litre of hooch tasting faintly of tomato but very sweet.

Another batch that we made out of apricots reeked, but tasted okay.

The funny thing was that Abdelrahman, who was the only true practising Muslim among the Nigerians, was the expert at making the palm wine. He didn't drink it, preferring to smoke hash. He said, 'At least I'm honest about it and not a hypocrite like these Afghan guards.'

10

Life after death

Throughout late 2010 and into 2011, while I was with the Nigerians in Block 4 of Pol-e-Charkhi, the focus of my case moved on to *ibra*, or restitution to the family of the victim. Leanne, from the embassy, had initially brought it up in our early discussions, but nobody in an official position explained it to me properly, so I gained much of my knowledge from fellow prisoners.

Ibra was a payment that the perpetrator of a crime made to the victim's family, but it was not a bribe or a guarantee of release. It was more a form of paying homage and doing honour than actual compensation in the sense that we in the West understand it. Afghans' concept of money is more complex, I think, than ours, or at least it operates on a different level. I remember one occasion while I was working for Four Horsemen, we had a client who owned a trucking company. We went out to visit him in the suburbs of Kabul, and although we knew we were paying him a lot of money and he was quite well off, he and his family lived in a typically primitive house with mud floors and rustic facilities. His son and a nephew stood by him with AKs, as bodyguards, to show what a big man he was. He showed us a galvanised iron trunk that was absolutely stacked with money: there must have been two or three million American dollars in there. He understood that money gave him power, but he was living in a hovel. He didn't make a connection between that money and how he could use it to improve his and his family's living conditions. Having power was the thing for him. The money was a lever that helped him influence other people. It had to be a visible thing, in cash, in that trunk. To spend it—on a decent house, even on basic necessities—would be to give away that leverage.

Similarly, the whole *ibra* process was about symbols and power rather than calculating a certain amount that Karim Abdullah's family had lost through his death and needed to live on.

I didn't get much of a sense of the family. I saw Karim Abdullah's brother, who was their representative, at the courthouse once, but we didn't have any interaction. The negotiations on my behalf involved Scotty, Dave, their fixer Karim, and Nathan, another member of the Bn who was in Afghanistan doing private security work and helping me in whatever way he could. With Karim as their interpreter, it was Scotty, Dave and Nathan who sat down with the family and negotiated directly over many months.

At first, the family didn't want *ibra*. We never knew if this was genuine or just part of the game where they claimed to be too upset or offended to take money, and just waited until we raised our offer. Around the time of my initial court hearing, they changed their mind and accepted an offer of US$20,000.

It might have stayed there until Jeremy Kelly's intervention. When he wrote about me for *The Australian*, the publicity indicated to Karim Abdullah's family that I was a very high-profile and valuable prisoner who might be worth a lot more money. Commander Haussedin's people stepped in at some point, as go-betweens on the family's side, and began to raise the ante. Bashir told Scotty, Dave and Nathan that there were going to be many more people who needed to take a cut, and the *ibra* amount began climbing.

Scotty, Dave and Nathan then came up with an excellent idea. How about Four Horsemen pay the *ibra*? The company had evaded its responsibilities when it came to looking after me through the criminal justice process, and had cut off all support. I was a dead man to them. But I was also a dead man who held a lot of their secrets. Besides, it was the right thing to do. Karim Abdullah and I had both worked for Four Horsemen, so surely they had some duty. On the other side of the negotiations, there was no resistance from Haussedin or his intermediaries to asking Four Horsemen. As Haussedin would be getting a cut from whatever *ibra* amount was settled, he was just as happy if it came from Four Horsemen's coffers, which, after all, he had been looting for years. It made no difference to him. By then, the *ibra* being demanded had risen to US$100,000.

The company finally agreed to pay, thanks to the intercession of Caleb, who had taken over as country manager. After working there he saw the same problems with the Macedonians as I had and was told by John Allen to fire Petar. Petar left, taking all the Macedonians with him. Because of the lack of staff, Caleb and Anton both had to be out on the road again.

Predictably, once Anton was back on the road he lasted about two weeks. One of the Afghan security men tried to kill him. The bullet bounced off his armour and went through his jaw, smashing it to bits. If Caleb, who spoke fluent Dari, hadn't been there, Anton would have died. And that was the end of Anton's war. Shot in the face by one of his own guys—that says a lot.

But thanks to Caleb and the persuasive powers of Scotty, Nathan and Dave, Four Horsemen was at least agreeing to pay the *ibra*. About a year after my third death sentence, Nathan and Dave came to see me in Pol-e-Charkhi and said, 'It's about to happen.' A court date was set, and I was driven back to the office where I had had my first hearing. The judge was the same Panjshiri guy, Baktiari, he of the big toenails. We had a much bigger attendance than at any of the hearings that actually put me in prison. The embassy representatives were there, as well as Scotty, Dave, Nathan, Karim and Bashir on my side. Karim Abdullah's brother was there with a retinue of go-betweens. And, again, there was Jeremy Kelly.

I said to the judge, 'I don't want media here. He's got to go.'

Through his interpreter, Kelly replied, 'Tell the judge I'm from the Australian embassy.'

It wasn't going to play for Jeremy this time—Chris, one of the embassy staff, who sported a blond mop of hair like Boris Johnson's, turned around and said, 'No, you're not.' As Kelly stormed out, Nathan's quiet parting comment was, 'Now fuck off, you little prick, don't let the door hit you on the way out.'

This time I sat there with a smug look on my face, and Dave and Scotty gave Kelly a little wave as he left. He still wrote an article about the hearing.

The *ibra* paperwork was handed up to the judge. Nathan had worked out how to make sure Karim Abdullah's kids got the money, at least on paper. But it was a tense few minutes. Anyone could say no and stop the whole process. They all want to be told they're important. That's why nothing ever gets done: they spend so long arguing over who's in charge. The judge made sure the documentation and the money were all there. A sheet had photos of the family members, who had all marked it with their thumbprints, saying they agreed to it. Then the brother, as family representative, signed it and I signed it, the court staff made duplicates, and that was it. It took less than half an hour. No arguments; bang-bang-bang, done, off you go.

I doubt the family received more than ten per cent of the $100,000. The *ibra* was, more than anything, a box to be ticked before anything else could proceed. On our side, it enabled us to dispense with some business. Karim, the fixer, had been decent at first, but recently had been ripping people off. He had got his last dollar out of my case. Bashir, who had been one hundred per cent useless since day one, went up to my mates after the *ibra* hearing and said, 'You owe me another US$5000.'

One of my friends said: 'How about I shoot you in the fucking leg?'

Bashir changed his mind, and we saw him no more.

The day after the *ibra* was paid, my sentence was commuted from the death penalty to twenty years in prison. Within a week it had been shaved back to eighteen years because of reductions I'd automatically received since my imprisonment under the Afghan prison system. Everyone knew that *ibra* alone wouldn't get me out, but it could stop me being executed. To be honest, though, I always thought being murdered in jail was far more likely than the death penalty being carried out, so I was hardly set at ease by the commuting of the death sentence.

The *ibra* hearing was also the last official dealing I had with Four Horsemen. By then it was about eighteen months since my arrest, and most of the people who had been at the company had left Afghanistan for good. I was told that when Scotty, Dave and Nathan were pressuring Four Horsemen to pay the *ibra*, Caleb had told John Allen that he had to help me after everything I'd done for him. I believe the money came directly from John. Just another wad of Afghanistan-bound cash, born of American guilt.

11

Saving lives

Towards the end of Ramadan in 2011, in the heat of summer, the majority of the prisoners, who were Muslim, were getting punchy. The stress of thousands of men not eating through the day, on top of the normal violence, frustration and personal antagonisms, turned the whole prison into a tinderbox. In the final days of the fast, they tore the joint apart and set fire to the mattresses and any other flammable material on their floor.

The prison guards' response, en masse, was to run away and lock the doors behind them. Leave the prisoners to themselves. Within a day, the Afghan rioters had taken over the jail.

The African crew and I barricaded ourselves into our floor. We gave no consideration to taking advantage of the guards' absence and attempting a break-out. Where would we go? We were in a dustbowl one hour's drive outside of

Kabul. There was literally nothing out there that was less dangerous than the inside. From my personal point of view, they didn't even need walls and gates.

The rioters were another matter. At one point they tried to break into our area, but we threw them back out. After they'd broken through the door we'd tried to block, Ken, Abdulrahman, Andre and I scrummaged them back. After we'd pushed them out, Richard managed to tie the doors closed again. Eventually a large group of police dressed in riot equipment turned up to quell things. They were the staff from Block 10, who had been trained by American prison guards under a US government program. They knew what they were doing, and knew that the hunger and fatigue that came with Ramadan, which had wound the rioters up into a fury, would also bring them crashing down. As the rioters began to tire, the police began clearing each floor. They were well trained and professional, shield-charging rioters into the wall, holding them there with their shields, dropping them onto the floor and zip-tying them, cleaning the place up.

The jail was now full of battered and bleeding inmates, but at that stage of my imprisonment I felt no desire to help them (not least because only hours before they'd been trying to break onto our floor). In the army I'd done a Combat First Aider course, and in South Africa on my Close Protection Course I'd gained a qualification as a Remote Medical Assistant. Later, I was more than happy to help other inmates, and found my first aid skill to be a genuine asset. I remembered John Allen saying that when it came down to it, this was how US Special Forces won people over, through their medics. There weren't many doctors in the jail, so I was the next best thing.

During my time in the security industry, there were a couple of occasions that stand out. When I was in Iraq, I was asked to help get an injured young girl out of a hospital. She had been adopted by an American, who was killed in a convoy not long after. With no family to look after her, she was left at the hospital in the Red Zone.

Our boss, Rob B, approached. He asked us, 'Can you go and find this kid off the books?' Rob B, with my close mate JT, another bloke called George, a hard-as-nails Parachute Regiment guy, and I were going to go into the Red Zone to get her out of this hospital and deliver her to the Americans. We began our preparations, but at the last minute Rob B told us the job had been called off.

I don't know what happened to the girl, and the frustration of that job stuck with me for years.

In Kabul, in early 2009, the opportunity to make up for that frustration presented itself. John Allen called me into his office at Four Horsemen and said, 'I've received this email from the military. You reckon you'd be able to do something about it?'

He sent me photos of a very young girl, about three years old, who had been taken into an American base at Khost, in the tribal highlands of eastern Afghanistan. She was badly burnt on her back and limbs. The doctors on the base had treated her as best they could, but she had to go to a proper burns unit, the nearest of which was at the general hospital in Kabul. Problem was, Kabul was a sixteen-hour drive away, over switchbacking roads in the Gardez mountain range, where you were a sitting duck for ambushes and attacks. Alternatively, Khost to Kabul was a couple of hours by helicopter, but the commanding officer of the base at Khost would not let the girl fly on a chopper. He said she was 'suspected Taliban'. A three-year-old girl. Right.

He did have his reasons. The girl's father had brought her into the base, and said she had been hurt in a drone strike. The back story to this was that Barack Obama, the new president of the United States, had announced a reduction in drone strikes, but instead stepped them up. To alleviate their guilt, the Americans offered financial compensation to the families of drone strike victims. Of course, the Afghans quickly cottoned onto how they could game this. Once they found out that Americans gave them money, they began burning their own children—only girls, mind you, because girls were worthless to them—and then turning up at the US bases with burnt daughters, supposed drone strike victims, looking for money.

The medical staff on the Khost base had a commonsense approach to how to deal with the girl. Sure, the father might have burnt his daughter in hopes of getting money, but at the end of the day she was a three-year-old with bad burns and you couldn't just turn her away. She had to get to Kabul or she would probably die. The Special Forces idea was that if you're good to the locals, they will eventually be good to you. This may seem obvious, but it was not always shared by the wider American military. John's SF friend on the base emailed him the photos of the girl and said it was shit that the CO hadn't let her fly out.

John saw how we could do something to benefit his company's, and our industry's, image. To get the girl to the hospital in Kabul would look better for Four Horsemen than what we were known for, which was driving around shooting at things.

'You think you can do it?' John said.

I said I'd give it a crack.

After seeing the pre-op photos and discussing it, Marcus Wilson and I both decided the air move would be better for the patient and safer for us. I rang around, and within half an hour had three helicopters I could get onto. At the beginning of my employment with Four Horsemen, I had received a 'white card', the pass onto American bases that gave me the equivalent rank to an officer. It was a very useful thing. If I got badly injured in a contact, the card meant I would end up on an American base in Germany to get fixed up. Having a US Department of Defence ID card opened doors for me within the bases. When I phoned around asking for seats on any helicopters going to Khost, people were more than happy to help, though it did freak me out when people called me 'Sir'.

Being with Four Horsemen could also open doors on the US bases, because some of the senior ranks, especially in Special Forces, knew John Allen and had worked with him. We were bringing them their mail from home, their supplies and fuel. Those who knew me respected the fact that I was game enough to wander around outside the wire by myself, protecting their mail convoys. They'd ask, 'Who do you work for?' I told them I was just a backpacker trying to earn enough money to get on the piss. They'd say, 'Yeah, good one.' I gave them information from being on the road that enabled them to clean up people they were after. They appreciated that. In return, if my guys got shot up, I could take them into a FOB and get free medical attention or ammunition, or time on their ranges to practise my shooting. The Yanks' patriotism can make Australians cringe, but they actually give a fuck about their country and believe they're doing the right thing. It can backfire on them a bit, which is a large part of why the world is in its current state. They have a naïve innocence to believe the world is fundamentally like them and wants them to go and help. They don't understand that cultures can be at a complete right-angle to theirs. They mean well, even if they've got no idea how their nation's actions impact on the world. When I made those calls to get onto a helicopter, I could rely on that goodwill.

I went to the State Department airfield with Frank and Marcus Wilson, who got onto a State Department helicopter that was to fly from Kabul to Khost. It was an Mi-17, an old Russian helicopter. Frank and Marcus were keen to help out. A humane thing for contractors to do, for a change.

When we got to Khost, the girl and her father were in the small base hospital. The father was wearing the *pakul*, the Pashtun tribesmen's hat which was often mistakenly identified as part of the Taliban uniform. The medical guys who were working on the girl agreed that he was a piece of shit, but not Taliban.

The girl was tiny, which made her injuries all the more heartbreaking. They were clearly burns from liquid, not shrapnel wounds, which was why the father's story about the drone strike was not believed. Later, the doctor in charge showed me other photos of children with similar burns. Always girls. I thought: *She's got no future, won't be married, burns like candle wax down her back and limbs. All for a few dollars that her fuckwit father has conned out of a stupid US policy.*

We could see we had made the right call about airlifting her back to Kabul. If we drove her on those bumpy winding roads, she would be in agony the whole way, not to mention us all risking our lives. So with the girl laid out on Marcus's stretcher, a big pink teddy bear cradled in her arms, we flew back to Kabul. She was in hospital for two weeks. Marcus footed the bill, and Frank and I got her back to her family. I'm sure they received the money. Nobody from the US government ever followed those things up, so you could guarantee it would happen again.

Frank and I, who were stoked with the whole exploit, went to the Gandamak, the pub where westerners congregated in Kabul, to meet Claire, the French journalist who was Frank's girlfriend. All fired up from our successful humanitarian mission, Frank said to her, 'Are you going to do a story on us?'

Claire looked apologetic. 'No one wants to hear good news about Afghanistan,' she said.

Later on in Pol-e-Charkhi, I helped any prisoner, no matter what they'd done. But I had to draw the line somewhere. The one group of patients I refused to help were not prisoners but the guards who would intentionally smash their hands in doors to get out of work. They would come to me for bandaging. I said, 'I'm helping other prisoners, not you. You go to town and sort yourself out.' In the way they begged for Band-Aids they were like children. When one of them had a Band-Aid they suddenly all wanted one. Any guard who had a Band-Aid would walk around holding his hand out so everyone could see. There was one cop who kept refusing to check on prisoners, refusing to do his job, because he said his hand was hurt. He wore Band-Aids with more display and pride than he wore his uniform.

Other medical incidents I was involved with in Pol-e-Charkhi did not end well, such as when I was called on to help one prisoner who had been stabbed with, of all things, a dustpan.

The Red Cross brought a care package to every prisoner in Afghanistan: blankets, socks, bedding, buckets and a plastic dustpan. One group of prisoners melted their dustpan down into a blob of plastic, and then sharpened it into a knife so they could stab another guy in the foyer of the block. When they were done with him, they called me and asked me to patch him up.

I looked at him lying on the concrete in a spreading pool of blood.

'He's dead,' I said.

'No, you've got to wake him up and fix him.'

I said: 'See that red stuff? That's supposed to be inside him.'

'Oh . . .'

So they got a wheelbarrow and took him off. They were made to clean up the foyer, which they whinged about having to do. The cops didn't take too long to arrest the main perpetrator, and I never saw him again. Cops had various ways of dealing with killings inside, which varied from complete indifference to handing out brutal beatings before charging the miscreant with the new crime. Minor incidents were mostly sorted out by the prisoners themselves, especially in parts of jail controlled by the Taliban.

It was actually horrible not being able to help someone, as happened with the biggest medical emergency I was called into.

Among the prisoners in Block 4, the only other white guy I got close to was the Russian Taliban fighter Andre, whom I've mentioned earlier. A foot taller than me, with a big beard, he had been conscripted into the Russian military as a young man. When he left the army, Andre said, he was drinking and doing drugs, until one day, in crisis, he went into a mosque in St Petersburg. The Muslim clerics got him clean and sober, and he converted within a month.

Due to his size and military background, the militant clerics eventually pushed Andre in the jihadi direction and he went to a training camp in Pakistan. It was probably run by Al-Qaeda, he said: they interviewed recruits as they came through, and if they were ex-military like Andre, they would be trained as fighters, whereas the rest went to suicide bomber school. 'Some of them were good,' he said, 'and others had no idea. They accidentally killed a lot of people during the training.'

Andre did so well that they were planning to put him in charge of a Taliban guerrilla group in Kabul after the war started. On his way into Afghanistan from Pakistan, he got stopped at a police checkpoint. The Afghans he was with had turned him in. That was the end of his war, before it even started. He hated Afghans now. They weren't true Muslims, in his view.

I had an interesting relationship with Andre. During my second winter in Block 4, we lost power for four weeks, after the transformer that supplied electricity to the entire jail blew up. Block 4 was part of the original Russian-built central 'wheel' of the jail, with walls that were two foot thick, but outside the snow was deep and the temperature was below zero even in the middle of the day. I was able to wrap myself up in some good gear that Dave had brought, including my Snugpak sleeping bag that I still had from when I was working for Four Horsemen. But to survive, everyone had to pull together more than usual. The Africans used to find wood and turn it into charcoal, which Andre and I used late in the night to boil water. That was the only way we could eat hot food and generate some warmth for ourselves.

We were both ex-military and we bonded through that and a shared liking for similar music.

One day, another non-Afghan prisoner, an old Ukrainian guy, had a stroke. He was an electrical engineer by trade, and kept himself in cigarettes and food by fixing any electrical problems that happened in the block. He was brilliant at it. As a former Soviet citizen, he had both Ukrainian and Russian passports. When he arrived in Afghanistan for work, the fact that he was carrying two passports made the police suspect he was a Russian spy and he was arrested at the airport. The company he was coming to work for dropped him like a stone and neither the Ukrainian nor Russian governments would do anything for him. He'd been in Pole-Charkhi for three years. It was a tragedy. And now no one but us could help him.

He'd collapsed in the morning and one of the Africans had come to wake me up to see if I could help him. It was obvious he'd had a stroke: half of his face had fallen in. I got Andre to come and translate for me, as at that stage the man was still conscious. We alerted the guards but they did nothing. For three days Andre, the Africans and I tried to care for him as he grew steadily weaker, pissing and shitting himself as he slipped into unconsciousness. Andre's mother, back in Russia, was a doctor, and Andre got her on the phone. The Ukrainian man was obviously dehydrated and needed fluids urgently. Andre and I had seen the Mark Wahlberg movie, *Shooter*, where he put salt and sugar into still water and made a drip. Having watched that together, we wanted to check with Andre's mother whether it would work. Through Andre, she told me how to make up the bottles and re-sterilise them, but while we were setting it up, the old guy died. He had been locked up for three years for a bloody passport violation, and he died on a dirty concrete floor surrounded by Andre and me, asking Andre's mother on the phone how to make a drip like we'd seen in a movie. Meanwhile the Nigerians were wiping his arse because he was shitting himself. What a way to go. And when he died, the Afghan guards said, 'There's no problem anymore, it's all good.' They didn't give a fuck.

The saddest part of it was that we'd managed to contact the Red Cross and they'd organised to get the old man out to a doctor. They arrived at the front gate but were denied entry by the guards for reasons we never found out. Ironically, after the old guy had died, the guards allowed the Red Cross to come and take his body for repatriation back to the Ukraine.

PART THREE

Survival of the Fittest

2012–2014

12

Mates

Maybe the worst thing that happened to me during my time in Block 4 didn't actually happen to me. In the middle of 2012, I heard on the news that my mate Didds had been killed by insurgents while on a patrol with the Australian SAS in Afghanistan.

To say I was gutted is inadequate. Sitting in an Afghan prison, when one of your best mates has lost his life just a couple of hours' drive away, gives you an unimaginable feeling of helplessness and hopelessness. You always wish you could have changed the course of history, even if you're only fantasising. But being in prison magnifies that feeling of impotence to the point where you feel literally crippled, unable to speak or move, almost unable to breathe.

When I'd first flown to Baghdad, on contract with Edinburgh International (EI), as a contractor for the first time after fifteen years in the army, I'd had some visa problems.

I was actually sent out to Jordan, where I had to wait overnight. When I went in the second time, I cleared customs and looked around the arrivals hall. EI had told me they were sending someone to pick me up. Unbeknown to me, those people had been stopped by an American convoy which had shot at their lead car.

I was standing in the terminal amid a large crowd, wondering what to do next, when I heard this Aussie voice say, 'What the fuck are you doing here?'

It was Didds. Although he was in the SAS, he was taking a year off from the army and doing some work for the private security company Olive, which had some big contracts in Iraq. This was not unusual for Special Forces types, as their skills are highly valued in the private sector. So here he was in Baghdad airport, waiting for a client.

We hung around for a while, talking shit, and after his client turned up, Didds said to me, 'Do you know these guys who are picking you up?'

'I know one of them.'

'Well, it's getting dark, you probably don't want to hang around the airport. I can give you a lift to the Green Zone and you can call them from there.'

To me, that made more sense than being alone after dark in the Baghdad airport. So Didds gave me a pistol and we jumped into his SUV.

While this was going on, the EI guys went to the airport and I wasn't there. They'd been shot up by the Yanks and now had to drive back in the dark, all for nothing. They weren't happy.

Once I got into the Green Zone, I eventually got through to the EI sat phone number I'd been given. By then, they were more surprised than annoyed.

'How the fuck did you get into the Green Zone without us?'

I told them I'd got a lift in because I thought they were a no-show, and having no point of contact at the airport I thought it was more prudent not to be left there. Later that night, they picked me up and took me to their compound and introduced me to everybody in the company. My airport non-appearance upset a few people but we laughed about it later, when they figured that the important thing was that I'd shown I wasn't the type to just hang around helplessly, and that I had friends like Didds who could make things happen.

As funny as Didds was, he was a lot more than that and had a key influence on my life. Back when I was still in the army and at a crossroads, I considered following Didds and trying out for selection in the SAS. I had put in for Special Forces selection a couple of times over the years, and some of my mates from the Bn were pushing me to do it. Several factors played into my decision not to do so, but one was a conversation with Didds, who said to me one night, 'Even for the [SAS] Regiment, you're a little bit too strange. If you see something you don't agree with, you won't do it. But over there, it's so political, you have to do things you don't like.' He knew me well.

When I heard about his funeral in Australia, it was tough. I got on the phone to Katie, and she went to the ceremony for Didds in his home town of Perth. Didds had been more than my mate. He was a friend of our family. When Katie went to the wake, she called me, and I was able to speak with several of my mates. It was good to feel that solidarity that we still shared, but I was gutted not to be there.

Camel and now Didds. I had to keep pushing on. Living is for the living.

Moving upstairs in Block 4 with the Nigerians had given me breathing space, a period of time to settle into safe routines in Pol-e-Charkhi and get some relief from the lurking sense that any day might be my last. The Nigerians gave me the solidarity and protection of numbers, a faction to be part of.

Even so, I was not one of them and nobody was under any illusions that I was. My habit was to hold myself back from people, a natural tendency since childhood that was accentuated when I was in prison. Abdelrahman and Ken were the closest to friends that I had among the Nigerians, but they were not really friends, more allies with whom I had a clear understanding and a way of peacefully coexisting.

The closest I had to a friend in my years in Pol-e-Charkhi was Bevan, who I met in October 2012 when all the foreign prisoners were consolidated in Block 10.

The Afghan government was shortening prison terms and gradually releasing the Africans and other foreigners through 2011, 2012 and 2013. In my gut, I didn't welcome any change. Although I was in a state of constant hopelessness about my case, and was pretty despondent all round, I felt safe enough in Block 4. I had a TV and DVD player and the rest, and knew that it was pretty rough in the other blocks. Block 4 was getting overcrowded; by that point there were more than 10,000 prisoners in the jail. They wanted to move us out because they were running out of room. We resisted the move until circumstances forced us.

In the second half of 2012, Paul Chigga was released from the prison after something like nine years. Andre left soon after, as did a number of other Africans. As there were fewer of us, it was easier for the guards to force us to move. Our new home was to be Block 10. It had been built with funds supplied by the British government as part of a counter-narcotics program specifically for housing those convicted of drug-related crimes. It sat in a separate compound outside the original Russian-built 'wheel', and by the time we moved there it housed all the prison's foreigners, as well as those sentenced to death, and a hardcore group of Taliban. The guards running Block 10 were in a different league. They were the guys who'd been called in to break up the riot the year before. We met the commander, a guy called Hershod, an Uzbek from northern Afghanistan, and his deputy Roz Mohammed. They were very tough but fair, and you didn't want to get on the wrong side of them. As an Uzbek, Hershod looked more Russian than Afghan. He was stocky, with forearms like Popeye.

Hershod proved his toughness when I got into a serious fight with a bunch of Afghan gangsters on the top floor of Block 10. They got the guards to sell them steroids, which weren't doing anything other than making them fat and emotional. One day, they paid the cops to get me out in the yard on my own so they could have a go at raping me. Rape was their hobby: they used to pay the cops to send young prisoners to their end, and you could hear the screaming and laughing. I imagined the scene in *Pulp Fiction* where Bruce Willis and Ving Rhames are tied up in that dungeon. It was unsettling, all the more so when you couldn't see what was happening. It reasserted two things I knew: the cops weren't clean, and 'Good Muslims' were not what they said they were. I wasn't horrified or scared, I just shook my head at the world I was in.

I was out in the yard for exercise, wearing shorts and no shirt, when five of these fat gangsters came out. I figured I'd been set up by the guards. One of the gangsters stepped up and tried to rip my shorts off. The others got me onto the ground, and one jumped on me and busted my ribs. It wasn't good. But a fight is a fight, and these guys were used to intimidating and slapping people around, not fighting with someone prepared to go the distance. Although I was injured, I was able to stand up again and take them on. They could see in my eyes that I was a bit wild and ready to clean them up. They could have overpowered me, of course, given their numerical advantage, but they were going to suffer some damage along the way. Once they realised it wasn't going to be fun and I wouldn't go quietly, they paused. Roz Mohammed and a couple of the decent guards soon appeared on the scene and pepper sprayed them before giving them a flogging and locking them in their cells for a couple of days.

Hershod put paid to this group after they set a fire in the jail, lighting up their mattresses. When the fire started up, all the guards ran outside and left the rest of us prisoners inside as black smoke filled the place. One of the prisoners rang Hershod, who was helping to sort something out in Kandahar. Within hours he flew back and went into the jail by himself with a baton and a radio. He beat the fuck out of the gangsters who had set the fire. We saw him talking on his radio, calling other cops in, in between smashing one of the gangsters with the butt end of that same radio. He'd already broken his baton on them. It was kind of funny. He dragged the perpetrators outside, handcuffed them to the fence, and ordered the cops to step up and beat the fuck out of them one at a time. As I said, you didn't want to get on the wrong side of him, but I found him to be fair and reasonable and we got on well.

In Block 4 we had been on the upstairs floor, but in Block 10 we were downstairs. On the floor above us, one side had

Taliban and Al-Qaeda prisoners, and on the other side were Afghan mafia, a catch-all phrase that we used for anyone who'd been involved in criminal gangs, arrested for smuggling drugs or arms, for kidnapping, and other crimes.

When I first arrived in Block 10, one of my cellmates was an English guy called Paul. Older than me, solidly built, Paul had left the British Army to work for a de-mining company before getting a job on a security contract. The Afghan partner in the de-mining company had committed tax fraud and skipped the country. Paul had been in charge of all the company's equipment and as his name was on certain documents that had been used in the fraud he was unwittingly swept up in it and found himself in jail. As fellow NCOs, he and I were like-minded and coped well by training, reading, finding something to do, and walking up and down the corridor talking shit. The whole time Paul was there, the British embassy didn't come once. I managed to get extra food brought out, so I could share with Paul and Bevan. The British embassy staff were known for their parties in Kabul. British squaddies couldn't get water for their guys in Helmand, a British guy in jail was abandoned, and meanwhile their ambassador had a weekly alcohol bill in the tens of thousands of dollars.

Paul soon got out, thanks to a brilliant American lawyer called Kimberley Motley, who was much better than the one I'd been given. Over the next few months, the remaining Africans were steadily released. Abdelrahman and Ken had people looking out for them on the outside, who organised the necessary bribes to secure their freedom. These were the dying throes of Hamid Karzai's term as Afghan president, and it was open season on bribes to free prisoners. Some Afghans who were in there for serious terrorism offences were out again within months, thanks to the government's willingness to take money.

As the more easy-going Africans were released, those that remained were a bad-tempered mob. We were living in the same section of Block 10, but the closeness that had existed in Block 4 was long gone. Tensions built up, and in the exercise yard, I got into an argument with one of them that tipped things over the edge. Since the fight with the Afghan gangsters, I had been locked in a separate fenced area by the guards when I went into the yard to exercise. I was working out with some homemade weights and this guy wanted to come into my section to use them. I told him he could have them in five minutes and the guard at the gate refused to let him in till then. He blew up at the guard, and Abdullah and two of the Ugandans piled in. A crazy fight broke out, spreading across the yard. The guards gave them a warning and then charged in with pepper spray. It ended with the Africans beaten and chained to the fence outside.

Roz Mohammed approached me in my cell soon after that fight and said, 'You have to come with me.' They wanted to separate me from the Africans to prevent further violence. I took what possesions I had and Roz took me across to the other side of the block. Getting moved was one of the best things that could have happened to me in Block 10, because it put me in with Bevan.

I'd first met Bevan when I moved to Block 10 and Hershod had brought him out to act as a translator. He had long grey hair, a tanned and lined face, and was five years older than me. We had hit it off instantly. Bevan was ex-military, from Pretoria. He was surprised by some of the names I knew from my time in South Africa, and we connected over a mutual love of his country. We always had a lot to talk about, both of us being military. Bevan had worked in intelligence and had a degree in political science.

Now, he sat up in his cell and asked Roz in Dari: 'What the fuck's going on?'

'He's living in here now.'

Bevan looked at me and quipped, 'You worked that well!'

'I didn't plan it, but here I am.'

Bevan had been arrested a couple of years before me, and was finishing his sentence when I arrived in the block. He had been sentenced to eighteen years for drug smuggling. 'I was guilty,' he said, 'in that there was a shitload of drugs in my bag.' At the time of his arrest, he had been third-in-command of SSSI, a security company. He said he believed he was transporting big bags of protein powder, but was sprung when the NDS were tipped off by associates of my old friend Commander Haussedin. When the NDS arrested him, they made him eat some of the drugs. 'I was off my tree for a couple of days,' he said. 'It was crystal meth, probably from China. I didn't know what it was or where it was from, but it was in my bag, so it was mine according to the law.'

Bevan had had a terrible time, not so much through abuse or punishment in jail but in what was happening on the outside. As a South African, his nearest consulate was in Pakistan, and no staff came to see him even once in his seven years in Pol-e-Charkhi. His mother died while he was in, his wife divorced him, and his father would die two weeks after he got out. I would see him hit a real low when his mum died, and I hoped and prayed, to whatever you pray to when you don't believe in a god, that my parents wouldn't suffer the same fate before I was released.

Bevan was interesting to hang around with and I learnt from watching him work people in his excellent Dari. The room we shared measured twelve feet by twelve feet, and in that confinement you get to know someone pretty well over a year. We got on the entire time, never having a falling-out.

Each of the cells in Block 10, which fed off a main corridor on each floor, was inhabited by two to four prisoners, whereas in Block 4 we had had an open area with a cage in the middle in which we had all slept.

In Block 10, each cell had a metal double-bunk, and either another double-bunk or a single. If you climbed on top of a double-bunk, you could look out the window of your cell into an open corridor that was outside—the police could walk this outer corridor during the night and check on the cells without actually coming inside the prisoners' area—and beyond that, the brick wall of the block, the paved concrete ring outside the wall, the chainlink fence encircling the ring, and out to the administration buildings, the kitchen building and the main office from which the prison was run. To the north of Block 10 was a visitors' area with some tufts of grass scattered patchily across the dirt. The level of maintenance was rudimentary at best, but mostly non-existent. The guards saw their responsibility as purely stopping anyone from escaping. Everything else was left to the prisoners, the overwhelming majority of whom couldn't give a shit. The life you made was down to you.

Bevan and I talked a lot about South Africa. Even though it was his own country, whereas I had fallen for it as an adult, we would both go back there in a shot.

I had gone there after leaving the Australian Army in 2004 and the attraction was instant. Not knowing what I wanted to do next with my life, I went to South Africa for a private security course and fell in love with the place. How I felt about South Africa was surprising, and hadn't been part of the plan. It might have had something to do with all the Wilbur Smith books I'd read as a kid. South Africa was the place for me—it got me from the start. I explored the country but made my base in Cape Town. South Africa has its problems and places that are dangerous, but I found the Cape to be a compelling mix of Newcastle, the Barossa Valley and Melbourne. And the cost of living was forty per cent less than in Australia. Craft beers for two bucks! South Africans had an attitude I liked. Without the comfortable Australian safety net of pensions and superannuation, if they want to make a go of things they have to graft hard and go out on a limb. They chase stuff and take risks rather than wait for someone else to sort their life out for them.

It was interesting for Bevan and me to compare notes on how many people we both knew on that military–private contractor trail through Australia and South Africa, through Iraq into Afghanistan. Ever since my arrest, I had been slowly joining the dots on Four Horsemen's involvement in stitching me up.

On the first day we met, Bevan had asked me, 'Did a guy called Kyle work for your company?'

I was suspicious. 'Yeah. Why?'

'You tell me a name and I'll tell you exactly what they were doing at your company.'

He didn't mean what they did for a job. He was fully clued up on the behind-the-scenes machinations and dodges. With his background, I believed what Bevan told me. The Macedonians had also worked for a company Bevan had worked for, and he knew exactly how they operated. Talking things through with him I began to understand how dirty the whole business was. I wasn't imagining that I'd been set up.

It was a turning point for me. My anger had a focus, and I became more determined than ever to survive this ordeal.

13

The beacon

Kimberley Motley was already a name in Afghanistan before she got involved with my case. An air force brat, Kim had an African-American father and a South Korean mother and, back in the day, had been a Miss Wisconsin. In the early 2000s, she went to Afghanistan to work on the Justice Sector Support Program (JSSP), a program set up by the Afghan government with American help to set up a functioning legal system. While she was doing that, Kim figured out that there were basically no decent lawyers in the country. So in 2008 she set up her own practice to represent people in Afghanistan.

My mate Dave, who had been one of Kim's security team leaders when she worked for the US government, had spoken highly of her ever since I'd been in the jail. He said she was one of the few people in the country with an understanding of how things were supposed to work and, more importantly, how they did work. She was the only western lawyer working in Kabul independently, and was in high demand from companies, the government and individuals alike. She had absolutely no competition.

While I was free in Afghanistan, I had bumped into Kim once at the Gandamak, while she was working on the JSSP program. Her involvement with that was one reason she knew the system from the inside out. Dave had first made Kim aware of my case in 2010, when we were negotiating towards the *ibra* hearing. He sounded her out about representing me. He and Scotty were still trying to work through Bashir, and were listening to his advice, and Kim didn't want to cross over with that. She also said she was incredibly busy getting her private practice up and running, but would keep an eye on anything that developed in relation to my case. Back in 2010, she had been good enough to come to the jail and tell me this herself. 'I want to help you in the long-term,' she said, 'but I don't necessarily agree with what the Afghan lawyers are doing for you.' At that stage, I had thrown my lot in with Bashir, whom the Australian embassy had recommended, and I hardly knew Kim, so we let it rest there. At the time, Dave and Scotty felt that Bashir was going to be able to swing it. I said, 'I'm going to have to go with my mates,' and she said that was fine.

For the year or two between the end of my *ibra* case and the evolution of my friendship with Bevan, I was incredibly low when it came to my prospects of release. I was rarely talking to Katie or my parents, and was just being kept alive by the company of the Nigerians and the visits from the embassy and Scotty and Dave. But even those became testy. Scotty and Dave would come in all pumped-up with news that my release was imminent. I got excited the first couple of times, but nothing happened and I couldn't get in touch with anyone. With limited communications, I let myself become isolated. When Scotty and Dave came with yet another reason for hope, I began to doubt them.

'Do you believe the Afghans you're talking to here, or do you believe us?' they said.

I didn't know what to believe, that was the problem. But to doubt them seemed ungrateful, as if I wasn't keeping up my end of the bargain.

For emotional sustenance, I was speaking to Belinda on the phone every day and we were talking about faith and hope, about political developments that might affect me and lead to a pardon. But everything was a false dawn, and each hope raised and extinguished was denting our relationship a little bit more. We were just going around in circles.

After I was moved to Block 10, I broke contact to a degree with Belinda. I lost faith in any kind of future. Faith is not all it's cracked up to be. It was fucking useless.

Katie was still there, and wrote letters to me or sent pictures that Maddie had drawn or painted that I could stick on my wall. When I had these periods of crashing, I could talk to my sister. She would just let me pour it out—it wasn't as if we could have conversations that began with, 'What have you been up to?'—and then she would gently steer me around to stuff I was interested in, like a movie I'd seen or a book I'd read. Once we had a long conversation about art deco architecture, of all things. That was Katie's way of bringing me out of myself.

I retreated, speaking regularly only to Bevan. I underwent a reorganisation of self, based on very simple questions. *What can I do? What can't I do?* I still got angry and pissed off and sad, but emotions were only going to break me. I had to place all my focus on things that I could change.

I saw Kim Motley for the first time in two years when she was visiting Paul in the prison. She had been the one behind his early release. He was only inside for six months despite having received a much longer sentence. She checked up on me, just in a decent human kind of way, to see that I was all right. I didn't see her again until one day out of the blue she turned up in Block 10 to see Bevan, who said, 'Do you want to have a chat with Rob on his own?'

We sat down and reviewed what had happened so far. Kim said, 'I think I can help you, but you've got to work with me.' That was fine by me. Scotty and Dave were leaving the country, and I had long since sacked Bashir. One thing concerned me, that was Kim's very high profile in the western media, which had done numerous stories featuring her. 'I want no media involvement,' I said. I still felt badly burnt by what Jeremy Kelly had done, and didn't trust any media. Kim agreed to that. In conclusion, she said, 'I've got nothing at the moment, but I will get you out. I can't tell you when that'll be. But I'm not leaving this country until I've got you out.'

Kim was putting great effort into Bevan's case. He had actually finished his sentence before I joined him in Block 10, but as 2013 wore on he was still in the fucking prison. Five or six times the guards came and got him. He packed up, we said goodbye, and he took his bags into town, thinking he was going to be released. Then at night he came back, time after time, demoralised. I'd say, 'Come on mate, don't worry about it, it'll happen.'

Bevan had fallen victim to the same open-market on bribes that had got the Nigerians out. The end of the Karzai era was just an open kleptocracy, insofar as it affected prisoners. Even though he had been due for release for months, Bevan was told that he couldn't finish his jail term until he paid a fine. A Panjshiri war lord who was inside the jail on drug charges with his son (they were notable in Block 10 for carting around a pigeon in a cage, so they could have the pleasure of locking up another living creature) had influence on the commission that reduced all sentences. They convinced the commission that Bevan was a fabulously wealthy westerner who should not be released until he had paid extra 'fines', of which they would take a cut. The Afghan government was forgiving fine defaulters, and if that was all those prisoners were in for, they would be set free. Despite the amnesty, the Nigerians were only freed after paying their fines, and this led the commission, who thought Bevan was wealthier than he was, to ask him for thousands of US dollars. The son of the war lord kept coming around to Bevan, telling him to pay. He refused, saying the decree had come through to forgive outstanding fines. The son said, 'But your fines are for something different.' Bevan still refused. He knew that whatever he paid, the war lord and his son would be pocketing some of it. By the end the demanded amount had fallen significantly, from fifty thousand down into the hundreds of dollars. It dropped each time he wouldn't pay, but he felt so strongly about it, he said he would not pay a cent!

Kim understood all the twists and turns of what was going on. She told Bevan he had to play this game, but she would make sure she got him out without having to pay. She tried to work with the South African government, who were not helpful, but eventually she got Bevan's name onto a list when Karzai released prisoners on clemency grounds. Kim kept demanding: 'Why is this guy still here?'

One day in late 2013, Bevan packed his bags for yet another trip to town. And then he didn't come back. I was in my cell alone, and I was absolutely stoked for him when he rang me that night to say goodbye.

Kim had come through. She'd said she would get Bevan out, and she did. This was proof that she got things done.

That made me the last westerner in Pol-e-Charkhi.

———

When I was on my own, I had special hiding places for valuables. With money, I would separate the notes out and slip them between the pages of my books, where the guards never thought to look. At one point I had US$500 in my cell, a fortune, and nobody knew. Intermittently I was allowed access to a phone, but I always liked to have backups and although it was harder to hide phones and phone chargers, I developed my own personal network of special hiding places around the prison, either in the dirt of the visitors' yard or in the vegetated area between the fence and the wall, where I would bury a phone or a charger in a plastic bag. Like a dog with buried bones, I would know where to retrieve them when needed.

One day around the time of Bevan's release, I dug up my phone and called Katie with what turned out to be an important announcement.

'I would never kill myself,' I said.

It knocked her over. Until then, we'd had periodic conversations where I said I was going to end it and she talked me out of it. She was always the optimist, while I was the 'realist'. If we had any conflict, it was because I thought she was too hopeful. But that was also her talent.

She was extremely pleased to hear it. This was the end of my feeling that I was going to die in that place. She said, 'I've never been concerned that someone else would hurt you, because you can always defend yourself, but I was concerned that you would hurt yourself.'

Not anymore.

When I received my first death sentence, I had no idea that I wouldn't be executed. I thought it was going to happen any day, and without warning. If I wasn't executed, chances were I'd be murdered.

It was after the second death sentence that I began to get a feeling that they weren't going to kill me. The system of condemning me to death on such meagre evidence, without me having a chance to properly defend myself, was so ridiculous, it was almost like the system couldn't make its own pronouncements with a straight face.

As we proceeded through the third death sentence and the *ibra* hearing, I began to understand that the system was more like a game with secret rules. You had to play it their way, but there were wheels within wheels and nothing was definitive. It wasn't ever as clear-cut as 'You will die' or, on the other hand, 'You pay a bribe and you will be released.' There were complexities, reflections of the way Afghans think and do business, and I had to set about learning them.

For me to see it as a game was also, I think, a hangover of army thinking. In my fifteen years in the Australian military, I would constantly be on the search for what the rules were and how to play them as close as possible to the line. I always did quite well in military law tests, working out ways around problems. Even with something as minor as haircut requirements, I managed to comply with the rules while kind of thumbing my nose at them at the same time. Once you know the rules, you can bend them. There's always a way.

When I got my head around the Afghan legal system as a game, I found hope again. I could only change things that were within my grasp. What kept me sane was focusing on those things, not on the things that I was powerless to change.

Bevan was a big factor in regenerating my thinking, by teaching me how to perceive the legal game and by getting me angry about the people who had put me inside. We couldn't let them win! But the biggest gift he gave me was to renew my connection with Kim Motley. After Bevan's release, I was stoked to have her represent me. I just had one big problem.

'I don't have any money anymore,' I said. 'Some of it got stolen, and the rest has been given away in bribes.'

'Don't worry about the money,' Kim said, 'I'll do it *pro bono*. Let's just focus on getting you out.'

Around this point, Dave and Scotty's company lost a contract and they had no reason to stay. They both returned to Australia for work reasons, having done so much for me. But it was probably better for Kim and the way she worked that she and I handled things directly rather than through go-betweens.

Kim would stick with me from 2013 right through to the end. We were similar characters, stubborn and hot-headed, and we often clashed. But Kim realised I wasn't just trying to wriggle out of something, and I wasn't full of shit like a lot of prisoners. She had secured the release of a South African whose situation was similar to mine. He had told an Afghan guy to put his gun down, and he didn't, so the South African had dropped him. The court agreed that it was self-defence but he still got seven years. His company paid *ibra* straight away, and he served about two and a half years before he was freed.

Kim took all my paperwork away—my court file, the records of interviews and judgments—and formulated a plan. She said, 'This is the way it's going to go. I am going to petition them to change parts of the law on foreigners under detention. We'll get the sentence whittled down bit by bit, and we'll get you an early release.'

'How early?' I said.

'That I can't say.'

I thought, *It's going to take forever.*

But it was already taking forever. The difference was, I had somebody in my corner who was going to give forever an end-date.

PART FOUR

PART FOUR

Strange Friends

2014–2017

14

Last man standing

The embassy staff were no longer coming to visit me, for security reasons. Two visits from Belinda had not lifted the stress, only aggravated it, and we had decided to give our relationship a break. I couldn't expect her to put her life on hold for someone she had only spent a few weeks with in freedom. While I was still getting visits from Ivan, my main outside contact was Kim Motley, but that too was stressful, with me nagging her for news all the time and Kim doing her best but not able to speed things up as quickly as I wanted.

After Bevan, I only shared my cell once, for a brief time, with Iqra, the polio-stricken Ugandan I'd known in Block 4. Iqra, his brother Zumi, and Derek, who acted as Zumi's body-guard, were the last Africans to be released, and I was not as friendly with them as I had been with Ken and Abdelrahman. Derek and Zumi were harassing Iqra over his devotion to Islam, so I told him he could come and share my cell.

He dutifully went to mosque and did Hazan at prayer times, and the rest of the time we talked shit on any number of subjects. Iqra was in prison for the same reason as a lot of the younger Africans: he did a drug run to build up a stake to start a business, and he got caught first time. I liked him because he was very smart and we got into massive arguments about religion. He was so rigorous with his prayer sessions that he eventually told me he didn't want to keep bothering me with his rituals, so he moved back with some Afghans and was released shortly afterwards. He was a good kid. I always had time for him.

After Iqra was released, I led a solitary life, surviving by setting routines for myself and following them with fanatical strictness. I would wake up around seven or eight o'clock in the morning, depending on how late I'd been up the night before. First thing was to make breakfast: porridge with some coffee. Ivan had brought me a plunger because sometimes I got half-decent American coffee, but otherwise it was instant.

I thought a lot about my time in the army, and I really believe that during this period, it was my army training that saved my sanity. When I was a young digger at Tully in Queensland, playing 'enemy' for three months in the scrub, I was with an old warrant officer who used to run the lessons. Sitting under a bush for days on end looking at nothing, you got used to mastering your boredom, but I was particularly interested in how this guy had overcome not only boredom but the trauma of battle. He was a Vietnam vet, having done two tours as a digger and scout and as a section commander. He fought with 1RAR at Coral-Balmoral. He said after the first day, when they'd been up all night shooting and were absolutely shattered, their nerves shredded to bits, their sergeant came around and said, 'Have a shave, get a brew on, clean your boots.' Once you're on task, you can deal with what you've been through. Practical tasks snap you out of the state of mind you've been in.

I'll never be a poster boy for the Australian Army, but when I was in prison, I was grateful for what the army had done for me. Just as soldiers deal with their trauma through daily routines, getting through the most difficult days one task at a time, my training prepared me for how to survive more than seven years of shit days.

Don't give up.

Make your breakfast, make your bed, clean your room.

Have lunch and train.

It was task after task after task. It's how soldiers cope. The army pulls your brain out and makes you almost OCD, so you're constantly on task and focused. It kills time and helps you through. It does make you crazy to live with, as some girlfriends have told me. Most of the time, the training I did and the tasks I set myself kept my emotions in check. When the OCD army shit kicked in, it shut everything else off and stopped the lid from boiling over. Instead of getting irritated with people, I saw everything as another problem to negotiate. The longer I was out of the army, funnily enough, the more this deep-seated mental training took over. It wasn't until I was in prison that I realised what a number the army had done on me: the desensitisation was meant to train you to come to terms with taking the lives of others, but here it was saving mine. They will never want me to advertise the fact, but when I was the last westerner in Pol-e-Charkhi, the Australian Army saved my life.

I gave myself jobs for the morning. If it wasn't washing my clothes or cleaning my cell, it might be reading, drawing or writing in the journals I had begun to keep. I read anything I could get my hands on, books brought in for me by Ivan or Kim or the Red Cross, or left behind by other prisoners. I'm a left-brain thinker, so maths is more difficult for me, but I challenged myself to read about mathematics and astrophysics, which was mind-bending. Eventually I would get to a point where I couldn't work things out because my maths wasn't good enough, but it was great brain exercise.

I can't remember not being a reader. Although we always had jobs to do as kids, my real interest lay in dreaming about the outside world and accessing it through books. Mum taught us to read when we were still very young, and books fired my curiosity. While the four of us kids at the station attended the School of the Air—the correspondence education conducted by radio lessons in those pre-internet days—my real education was in the books I read. I was only any good at schoolwork because I read so much, I could figure out grammar and punctuation. Our lessons had been written in the 1950s and there was a big emphasis on those nuts and bolts of writing, which had become second nature to me.

I was always keen to knock off my twenty minutes on the radio and my hour of homework before getting on with my own interests. We had no television, so the library books that would turn up after Mum visited the nearest large town— Port Augusta, 300 kilometres away—and the paperbacks swapped among the adults and children were my meat and drink. I read everything, and reading made me different. I grew up thinking I could do what I wanted with my life, and that meant getting away from South Australia, escaping into the worlds I was reading about.

As it turned out, I got away sooner than I was ready when I went away to school at Woomera as a twelve-year-old.

Leaving home at such a young age increased my self-reliance and independent outlook. When I was fourteen or fifteen I started reading the German philosophers Friedrich Nietzsche and Martin Heidegger, and got right into the idea that man evolves by breaking himself down and making himself better. Nietzsche's idea of the *ubermensch*, or superman, had been misappropriated by the Nazis in Germany but I didn't know about that; what I read was an ideal of betterment. We all have the capability to do things better and to make great things. Humanity has the potential to improve, whether it's through some technological marvel such as developing a satellite that can fit on an ice chip in space, or simply through someone like me thinking of better ways to get my work done or, when I was in the army, coming up with ideas for how to improve the organisation of my platoon. Self-improvement was always in the front of my mind, and this idealism was what got me through those solitary years in my teens.

When I looked back from prison, I recognised that the way I grew up prepared me for army life when it meant going bush and doing field exercises. I liked being on my own, I grew up on my own, I felt I could learn stuff on my own. I never realised it, of course, but in the open spaces of the Australian outback I was also developing the kind of personality that was pretty well adapted to the job of survival in the claustrophobic confinement of an Afghan prison. Drawing was also something I'd enjoyed since I was a kid, following Dad's example. My daily routines in jail often set aside special periods for both reading and drawing. My journals were mainly mundane records of my training programs on any given day, or repair jobs I was working on. *Fix toilet, fucked again at four in the morning.* Next day: *Toilet still not fixed, so fixed again.* Next day: *Broken again.* I recorded visits from Ivan or Kim, and important dates such as Anzac Day or Christmas.

My staple lunch was either bread or something better if Ivan or Kim had brought food in. They had got me a smartphone, and after lunch I would browse the internet, following tangents, keeping up with the news of the world. The internet was a blessing for me. I would hear about something on the radio, then chase it up online, following story after story, and suddenly I could look up and the afternoon was gone. One more day down without going insane, chalk that up as a win.

By 4pm, the guards would open my cell door and I would do my training. I had a whole program of push-ups, pull-ups on a bar outside my room in the internal corridor, heaves and leg raises. Exercise was my therapy, and mostly I did it in my room because nobody would bother me there. It freaked out some of the prisoners and guards that I got big and strong while rarely leaving my cell.

When I did go outside, it was to run a couple of laps around the entire block. There was a strip of concrete between the walls and the outer fence, and the guards allowed me to run that circuit, which was about four hundred metres all the way around.

After exercise, I had a wash. My cell had an alcove bathroom with a shower, but the shower didn't work. I paid to have a hot water element brought in, but some of the prisoners upstairs heard about it, and paid the guards a removalist's fee. After one day, my hot water element was taken to those prisoners. Oh well. I went back to washing myself with water that I boiled with an immersion heater.

My evening routine would begin with dinner preparation: cut up my vegies, cook some meat if I had it. I would break down the preparation, as I broke down the whole day, into separate small tasks. It's surprising how you can fill your time when the day becomes a sequence like that. I am a bit of a perfectionist, a habit that developed during my time in the army, and it grew into an obsessiveness and compulsiveness in prison so that I was in a kind of Zen state trying to get every part of my dinner cut up and cooked exactly how I wanted it.

I would eat at six or seven o'clock in the evening, which was a lot earlier than the Afghans. After my dinner, I would interact with prisoners or guards: talk shit, or help them out with their English, which a lot were working on. When they went off for their dinner, I would have one more cup of coffee and go outside to breathe in some fresh air for the last time in the day. Then I would read, watch a movie when I had a television, and crash out.

When I'd been moved from Block 4 to Block 10, I had lost most of my possessions, including the TV and DVD player. Once I was on my own, after Bevan left, I gradually built up my effects again. To get a TV, I wrote letters to the head of the prison. The authorities would agree and then renege. 'We can't let you have one, because no one else does.' That was bullshit. I kept writing. At one point I managed to take a photo of TV antennas stacked on the prison roof with a phone that I borrowed, and I sent the photo to the Australian embassy.

After the embassy mentioned the number of TV antennas on the roof of Block 10 to the general in charge of prison, he finally relented and a TV turned up, courtesy of the very kind Werner Groenwald, an Afrikaaner pastor, and his wife Hannelie, a medical doctor, who were in Afghanistan working for an NGO. They believed their mission in Afghanistan was to bring more than just aid; they wanted to spread the word of God. Since 2002, Werner and Hannelie had lived in Afghanistan and raised a family there. Werner had left a big congregation in Pretoria and Hannelie had been running an emergency room until they decided to go and help others in Afghanistan. They got to know me through Bevan, and, after he left, they visited me once a month without fail, bringing all the food sent from Australia via the embassy, even though they had no reason. They never banged on about the Bible—the most they would do was end a meeting with a group prayer—and they never judged me, always remaining positive. After Marcus Wilson left the country around 2012, Hannelie took it upon herself to make sure I was healthy and to look after me when I got sick, which, fortunately, wasn't too often. They were really heroic people and I owed them a huge deal. Tragically, Werner and both of their children were murdered by Afghans wearing police uniforms in 2014, one of the shittiest things that happened in that whole shitty time. The one saving grace was that Hannelie wasn't with them and survived.

The TV they gave me was an old one, but the guards pulled it apart to search it. I got local channels on it, but it was never right after the guards tampered with it. Later, I was able to get an LCD TV with a free-to-air digital box showing seventy channels. Having the news channels made an incredible difference, and there would be a new movie on every night that I hadn't seen. The best news channel was RT, the Russian channel—as long as they weren't talking about Russia.

I got that LCD TV through once again applying constant pressure on the prison authorities, with the help of the embassy. The Australian government and DFAT did all that they could on my case from what I could see, within the restrictions of their policies, but people at the embassy whom I'd never met would prop me up when I was having a bad day, sending in supplies with the Groenwalds or just checking out that I was okay, and they fully backed up my determination to get something I wanted. I would push and push and push. I had specific aims every month. It took me two years to get a kettle bell for training, but I got it in the end. I wrote letters, worked the rules, played everything in the bureaucratic game. Little wins like that did a lot for my morale, even if they didn't mean that much on their own.

A lot of my routines were aimed at improving the material conditions of my existence. No matter how small, it was worth doing. Originally, my cell had synthetic blue carpet over the concrete floor, and this carpet was ugly, smelly and hard to keep clean. It did nothing to maintain warmth—the cell didn't get horrendously cold because Block 10's walls were two foot thick and there were heaters installed in the corridors. So I pulled the carpet out, and, like any home renovator, I felt good about that.

Every second day, I swept and mopped the floor of the section of corridor directly outside my cell door and took the dust off the top of the heaters. Afghan prisoners or guards would come to the cell and watch me.

'Why are you doing that?' they said.

'I like it to be clean,' I replied, thinking: *Fuck off.* In my mind, my cell and the small section of corridor outside it were 'Australia' and the rest of the block was Afghanistan. I kept my country clean.

As well as the floors and the heaters, I cleaned the tops of my doors and windows. That blew the Afghans away. They would stand and watch and shake their heads in amazement . . . and then spit on the floor. Not to aggravate me, just because that's what they did.

Because of the thickness of the walls, it didn't get too hot in summer. I sliced up some foam mattresses and blocked off the windows in my toilet and my room, which cut down the light and the dust and also kept me a lot cooler. If I wanted more air flow, I would open a crack in the matting and let it blow through. It got still, but I never found it too hot unless I was exercising.

I was able to cut the mattresses with the knives I made from bits of metal and wire I found lying around, and secreted in different places around the block, both outside my room and inside, so I knew I would have access to a weapon if I needed it. I asked a cop for a proper knife, and he went to Hershod, who agreed to give me one to cut my food. That was the only knife I stashed in my room. It was just a piece of strip metal with wood wired to it, sharpened on the concrete floor, but it did the job. I never had to fight with it. The best cure for knife wounds, I had learnt, was avoiding getting into fights.

In my first couple of years in prison, I had become angry and emotional about things, but as I went on my emotions were cauterised. In my increasing solitude, I grew numb. Sometimes other prisoners would irritate me, such as when they tried to plug four heaters into the one powerpoint and wondered why the electricity stopped working. I said, 'This is why it's not working: you're not supposed to draw down that much power off those wires.' They just looked blankly at me and said, 'But it's meant to work.' I tried to get the guards to fix it, but they fucked it properly. It was like working with children. One guy's actions cut the power to the whole block for two days, and the prison had to change the fuses.

But now, instead of letting my irritation blaze away and end up in a fight, I kept my focus on what I could do, practically, for myself. I managed to wire my appliances by taking my room's wiring apart and working out which was which. I eventually got a powerboard sent in from the embassy and ran everything off that: television, stove, kettle. Another victory. This was what my world had come down to.

15

The Taliban and I

My biggest worry, during my last three years in Pol-e-Charkhi, was that the country would descend into chaos and discipline in the prison would get so bad that I couldn't defend myself. Sometimes the control of Hershod and Roz Mohammed was the thin blue line between the stability we had and an outbreak of anarchy.

When the Americans began their military withdrawal in 2013 and the presidency passed from Hamid Karzai to Ashraf Ghani in 2014, there were heightened fears that Afghanistan would fall apart again. If that should happen, my greatest hopes of safety lay, ironically, with the Taliban. Due to the ties I had made with Pashtun fighters before my imprisonment and what I had observed of the mostly Pashtun Taliban since I had been inside, I trusted them more than the gangsters and kleptocrats who were in power.

The Taliban mufti I got to know in jail, Hakemi, told me before his release, 'When the Taliban get back into power, look for me. I will personally drive you to the airport and put you on a plane out.' I believed him. Hakemi never lied to me. Some of the anti-Taliban prisoners got into me for that, harassing me for my friendship with Hakemi, but I was honest and told them that I trusted him more than I trusted them. That pissed them off.

It also pissed off Katie when I told her I had made friends with a Taliban mufti. She absolutely lost it.

———

I was always interested in the bigger picture. I think that curiosity and awareness made me better at what I did. I was never a robot: 'Walk up this hill, keep your head down and follow orders.' If you don't understand why you are fighting a war, what good are you? You're just a mechanism for a rifle.

Throughout my life, I have always inquired into other cultures, trying to work out why people do the things they do. Our times have raised these questions over and over again. When the Twin Towers came down on 11 September 2001, I was on leave from my job as an instructor at Singleton, at my house, preparing to go back to work the next day. My girlfriend at the time, Jules, was at work at the Rio Tinto mining site. She called me and said, 'Put the TV on right now.' I turned it on just in time to see the second plane hit. I went straight to work that night. Everyone was locking the place down, getting into a state of preparedness, even though the threat at the time was very small.

I didn't think immediately that Australia would get involved, but the Special Forces were in Afghanistan within weeks. I met some of those guys who were on the first deployment a few months later, when I did a promotion course, and we talked about the wider causes and repercussions of this new 'war on terror'. It still looked as if Special Forces were the only Australian soldiers who would be involved. For it to get to the point where infantry battalions went over, the war would need to get bigger and bigger.

My departure from the army into private security actually hastened my involvement in the Middle East. I went to Iraq a year after George Bush's bright idea to depart from the war on Islamic terrorism and invade Iraq instead. Everyone who was close to the scene in Iraq knew that the possibility of Saddam Hussein having 'weapons of mass destruction', which was the pretext for the invasion, was a stretch. But I guess the whole world came to know that eventually.

Going to Iraq gave me a chance to see how the Americans ran a war, and it didn't bode well. They eventually poured more than a trillion dollars into the country and it only got worse. Similar could be said for Afghanistan, where the Americans redirected their main efforts from 2008. Their strategic aims were never clear. Was it nation building, and, if so, whose bright idea was that? The change of mission was confusing to everyone. On the ground, when soldiers talked about the bigger picture, they had little idea what they were actually there for. They could identify and execute their day-by-day tasks, but as for strategy, forget it. I never met anybody, at any level of the military, who had any clarity. From a war-fighting point of view, the lessons of Vietnam had gone unlearnt: yet again, the West was going into a war with one hand tied behind its back, restricting what its soldiers could do, not allowing them to fight by the same rules as the enemy. They were never sure if they were fighting a war, building a nation, securing 'democracy', or just trying to get out of the place as safely and as acceptably, in the political sphere, as they could.

The war had been started, like all wars, by politicians on their last legs with their testosterone running out. Then, like all wars, it was being fought by young men full of testosterone. The old men are showing they've still got it, and the young men are showing they have it in the first place. If you can sort that out, without giving everyone vasectomies, the world would be a better place. But once they were there, if they weren't prepared to fight it properly, they should have got out.

This mess created an enormous vacuum, a perfect environment for companies like Four Horsemen and war lords like Commander Haussedin to siphon off some of the enormous flood of money coming into Afghanistan. If the politicians had wanted to create a situation where gangsters and corrupt private businesses could run this war for profit, they could not have done a better job.

How do I summarise my personal experience of the war? I wanted to know, I went and saw, I found I was good at what I did, and I enjoyed the adrenaline of being in fire fights. I didn't have to worry about anything else, as the world was reduced to the present. But putting back together people who'd been shot to bits, with that burnt-rust smell of blood, was horrible. Afterwards, I would be stoked that I'd got through each contact, but that elation was mixed with the images of those who hadn't, such as a truck driver who had had half his jaw shot away. I was trying to put an airway through, the kid next to him was screaming, and he ended up dying anyway. It didn't leave me horrified or suffering from nightmares, but the overall effect was a residue of weariness. I would feel burnt-out and lacklustre.

Despite all my frustrations working there and then the shit of my years in prison, I have a great fondness for Afghanistan. I would go back there now, if the situation was more stable, just to have a look around. It's an incredible country. The towers on the road to Kandahar have stood there for more than a thousand years. Not many places have that kind of history, which is pretty cool considering today's Afghans struggle to build a house that will last ten years. There's a stark beauty to the deserts and mountain passes. In wintertime at night, when there was no fighting, I could travel around freely. I drove around just looking, and when there was snow on the mountains it would throw as much light under the moon as an eerie daytime.

Even before my connection with Commander Mansour and our crew, I found the Pashtun tribe, from whom the Taliban sprang, to be good people. If you are invited into their house, you are protected by Pashtunwalli, the system of manners that dictated that once you have accepted a guest into your home, he becomes as precious as family. When I got to know Mufti Hakemi in jail, he told me that he was not happy after September 11, because he could see that the Taliban would protect Osama bin Laden, not so much for ideological or religious or even financial reasons, but because of Pashtunwalli. They would not hand him over. So the Americans would come for him and them. Hakemi said he saw that from the start, and it never pleased him.

When British Paul first came to Block 10, a group of young thugs who were in for the kidnap and murder of a ten-year-old would abuse Paul for wearing shorts. They'd been sentenced to death in their first court hearing, and hoped that showing themselves to be pious would help their case. They'd yell, 'You can't wear shorts in front of us! We're good Muslims!'

Paul would reply, 'Yeah, that's why you're in here.'

On one occasion they came close to the gate separating our corridor to shout abuse at us. I grabbed one of them by the scarf that he was wearing and bounced his head off the bars. That drove them wild and they threatened to kill us. These prisoners, even if they talked about being 'good Muslims', were not Taliban, just scumbag criminals. Pretending to be religious did them no good in the end, and when they were taken off to be executed, they sobbed and shat themselves and begged for forgiveness.

Genuine Taliban were different and I rarely had a problem with them. Even when they had to die, they did so with dignity. Sentenced to hang, Taliban prisoners said to the guards, 'Get your hands off me,' and walked to the gallows under their own steam. I could respect that.

I met Hakemi when I was in Block 10, although I had been aware of him, in my peripheral vision, when I was in Block 4 with the Nigerians and Ugandans, some of whom he was instructing in religion.

When you are going through shit like this, you don't necessarily become friends with someone from 'the other side', but you establish working relationships. The Russian Taliban Andre and I were able to talk together, to appreciate music together, and, while we were treating that old man who'd had the stroke or boiling water in winter or talking about the war, to put aside the fact that if we were outside we would have been trying to kill one another. These are the strange fellowships you make.

Andre had been taking religious instruction from Hakemi, but it was only when the Russian was released, after he'd been in for ten years, that I met the mufti properly. Aside from Andre, I had steered clear of the Taliban prisoners, not wanting to get mixed up with them since I had given that guy in the toilet a kicking.

When I went to Block 10 and the prison consolidated all the remaining non-Afghan prisoners there, including the last handful of Nigerians and Ugandans, Hakemi was teaching Iqra, who wanted to continue his study of Islam. The other two, Derek and Zumi, told Hakemi that they didn't want him in their cell, and stopped him from coming in. British Paul and I said to Hakemi, 'You can use our room as a mosque with Iqra. We'll fuck off and walk around the hallway, and when you're done we'll come back and drink coffee and talk about things.'

It was interesting to talk to Hakemi about how the Taliban saw the world. It reminded me of conversations I had had with Mansour. When I looked at it from their point of view, what they were doing made sense. I was interested in the tactical approach they'd taken, and also why they were fighting. All they wanted was for everyone else to leave so they could run the place. Which I could understand. Hakemi was a smart dude who had read Che Guevara's *Guerrilla Warfare*, among other military books, and understood the big picture: he said the Taliban would have been crushed if the Americans had kept at them in 2002 and 2003, but, by getting interested in Iraq, they had let them off the hook.

For all his insight and reason, he still subscribed to a shit ideology with shit ideas of how things should be run. What the Taliban did to women and children is wrong. The fact that they want to live in the thirteenth century is wrong. Did I like them? No, I hated every single one of them. But once I understood their perspective, I did respect them. Hakemi was good to talk to because he was well educated, he had a brain and a sense of humour. But he was Taliban. And if we were on the outside, I'd kill him. It's weird.

As well as being a mufti, Hakemi had become a mullah when he was twelve and memorised the Koran. That was pretty much all that was required to be a mullah, he said: there were young mullahs who could recite the whole Koran in Arabic without being able to speak a single word of the language in conversation. He, on the other hand, was fluent in both written and spoken Arabic. He came from the Kabul area but he dressed like a Pashtun, which the Taliban predominantly are. Considering where he came from, he was widely travelled and had been to India and Turkey before he was arrested.

Hakemi thought he was thirty-one or thirty-two when we met, so he had spent his twenties growing up amid the war until he was arrested by the NDS on terrorism charges. For the Taliban resistance, he seemed more of a planner and a religious teacher than a fighter. He was an abstract thinker, who wondered out loud about how to involve women more in Taliban society without breaking the boundaries of strict Wahhabism. He had several sisters and unusually tried to see the world from their perspective.

His English was good, but one of his idiosyncrasies was to call everything a 'system'.

'So,' I said, 'when you get back into power, it will be the slaughter system?'

'Are you making fun of me?'

I laughed. 'No, man, why would you say that?'

Then he opened up his notebook and began writing.

'What are you writing?' I said.

'Note to self: fatwa against Mr Langdon.'

'No, man, don't do that!'

He looked up with a straight face that broke into a smile. He was pissing about, and we both had a laugh.

We constantly bantered like that, between serious and light-hearted, often with a bit of an edge. Hakemi explained Sharia law to me, and then how it worked in Afghanistan. He asked me about my case.

'Have you paid the *ibra*?'

'Yes.'

'If we were in power, you would now be free to go. It's either your life or cash. If the cash has gone to the family, you get your life back. The debt is settled.' But Afghanistan's legal system, such as it was, was a mishmash of western and Sharia law, which meant the *ibra* was only a gateway to sentence reductions. Hakemi helped me understand that, which was good, because the interconnection of western and Sharia elements in their legal system had been bewildering and frustrating to me for a long time.

He looked on it as his duty to try to convert the western-ers. As he put it, he liked us and wanted us to be brothers in Islam and not just friends. Pol-e-Charkhi was a factory for making Taliban. Prisoners who had nothing to do would go to the mosque, and who ran the mosque? The Taliban. Who looked after prisoners when they needed a problem sorted out? The Taliban. Who maintained a modicum of order? The Taliban.

Hakemi struggled to understand why we wouldn't convert. At one point Bevan and I were talking about me starting a university course by correspondence from Australia.

Hakemi said, 'Why can't you just sit there at peace?'

'I want to make use of my time,' I said.

'Why don't you learn Islam?'

But he knew I was no more interested in becoming a Muslim than in doing drugs or taking up basket-weaving as a means of taming the boredom. A long time ago I decided I was an atheist. Religion is responsible for too much bad shit.

That said, I am interested in what religion means to those who take it up or already have it. I don't have anything against religious folk, and have known people whose lives have been cleaned up by a commitment to faith. For one friend of mine with an addictive personality, her born-again Christianity was a far healthier addiction than what she was doing before.

This curiosity was what kept drawing me back to discussing Islam with Hakemi. I had taken an interest in Islam ever since I was in East Timor, trying to make sense of what the Indonesians were doing (I concluded that their occupation of the island had nothing to do with God, and everything to do with military muscle). Over the years, I had examined the different sects of Islam, which I discussed at length with Hakemi. I argued that some majority Shi'ite Islam countries had been more reasonable than Sunni-dominated countries in their human rights records, and Hakemi didn't dispute that in many ways conservative Sunni states, financed by Saudi Arabian Wahhabi Islamists, were at the root of much of the death and destruction in the Middle East. It was obvious to me that fundamentalism was the issue, and not whether a group were Sunni or Shi'ite. 'Look at the Kurds, who are Sunni,' I said. 'They have women fighting alongside the men. In Jordan people treat each other as equals, at least compared to what they do in Saudi Arabia.'

To his credit, Hakemi didn't put any fatwas on me and he was always open to discussion. From his point of view, these conversations were not a way of winning me over or converting me, but just his means of dealing with the world and with the boredom of prison life. And yet, his reasonableness didn't hide the fact that he belonged to a group who condones the stoning of women accused of adultery, whether the accusation is substantiated or not. In Afghanistan, when people had power, they would do what they wanted and exonerate themselves by saying it was God's will. I'm pretty sure it wasn't.

———

What I found even more interesting than the religious discussions was how the Taliban operated, as a group, in the prison's power system. Their area, upstairs from us in Block 10, was spotless. Everybody else lived like animals, but the Taliban assigned clear daily tasks and were organised rigidly, like the army when I first joined it at Kapooka. When Bevan and Paul were still inside, they invited us for some meals and were extremely polite, sharing food with us, even though they knew who and what we were. Bevan was able to translate their Dari conversations for our benefit.

They had satellite phones up there, and ran operations on the outside. On one occasion, we were sitting in their area eating and talking with them when their phones started going crazy. They said to us courteously, 'Mr Robert, Mr Bevan, can you please leave the room? We have a discussion to have.'

One of the Taliban commanders admitted to us, 'We're pretty sure the Americans are not going to bomb this place. We can run operations from in here forever.'

In Middle Eastern societies, what people say and what they do are often different, and this is accepted on both sides as an avenue to survival. I would watch Hakemi play non-Talib people off against each other and wonder why they couldn't see it coming. He was a master. The Taliban could organise the payment of money to get cases changed from terrorism to drug charges, and their people would receive reductions and releases. Inside the jail, the Taliban were an effective alternative government. They didn't start fights inside Pol-e-Charkhi, but they paid or told people to start them in certain blocks. Then the police would come to the Taliban and say, 'We can't stop this fight. Can you help us?' The Taliban would go in and mediate, and get something in return out of the police. They did it all the time. They were great at massaging situations to their advantage. That's pretty much how they operated in the outside world too.

Every now and then, someone senior in the Afghan government would crack the shits about the Taliban having too much control in the prison, so there would be periodic attempts to shut them down. It never came to much. The cops were fundamentally lazy—'What, you want us to actually work?'—and unwilling to tamper with a system that maintained order without any effort from them. That too was a reflection of the world outside. At every level, the Afghan authorities would do business with Taliban guys, because business was different from war.

There was an operational commander from Hakemi's group who I nicknamed 'Triple J' because his favourite expression was 'Jung, Jung, Jihad!' which meant 'Fight, Fight the Jihad!' Sometimes we could sit and talk to him— he spoke in Pashtun which another guy translated into Dari which Bevan translated into English for me. Triple J's reputation often stopped problems before they happened. One night, the gangsters who set the jail on fire were playing their radio too loud. Triple J said, 'We're praying here, can you turn it down?'

They told him to fuck off.

'Okay,' he said, 'I'm going upstairs to get my friends, we'll ask the police to unlock the doors, and we'll come and turn it down for you.'

It stopped at that point. He was the real deal, one of the few Afghans I met who fought with his hands, not just with an AK. He was scarred and wiry, and frighteningly quick.

Hakemi knew I wouldn't convert, but he had to have a try. I challenged him, saying, 'You don't want me to convert, you want what's inside my head.'

They knew that I had worked with Mansour and his Pashtun mercenaries outside, and had heard of my good reputation among them, and that was enough to secure protection for me in the jail. But they wanted more, of course.

Hakemi said, 'You're a communist, same as the Russians.' To him, 'communist' was interchangeable with 'atheist'. 'You're not going to convert. Why don't you work for us? We'll pay you.'

I said, 'You couldn't afford me, mate.'

Which wasn't true. They had tens of thousands of American dollars upstairs for bribes, smuggled in by visitors and corrupt police. They could definitely afford me, but for religious conversion I wasn't for sale.

Instead, Bevan and I kept our eyes and ears open because every so often we'd hear something interesting that we could pass on to the outside. For example, Hakemi showed us videos on his phone of Russians teaching the Taliban unarmed combat in Pakistan, and Irish guys teaching them how to use .50-calibre semiautomatic rifles—weapons that were old IRA favourites.

When a big insurgent attack happened on the outside, I could ask Hakemi directly if that was his group, and he or other Taliban guys were happy to confirm it or not. I don't think they suspected me of spying; they were unable to suppress their pride in what they'd done.

The Taliban were people you could work with, but one of the enemy in jail was of a completely different magnitude. Dr Jamal had been imprisoned for an attempted hit on President Karzai in 2011. In his late forties, a doctor, psychologist, and fullblown Al-Qaeda, the dude freaked me out. He sent me a letter about converting and I forwarded it to the embassy. They were more horrified by him being in there than what he'd said. Their reply was, 'What, you're in with people like that?' There was no threat in his letter, but while it appeared to be perfectly rational in the way it was expressed, there was an underlying insanity to it that disturbed everyone who read it. I saw him brainwash people who'd come in on drug charges so that the next thing they were out on the streets blowing themselves up. He got in their heads and twisted them around. An idiot with a gun is one thing, but a fanatic with that level of intelligence who really knows what he's doing is scary.

The dynamic among the Taliban in prison changed in the second half of my jail term, after Osama bin Laden was killed and the Taliban leader, Mullah Omar, was revealed to have been dead for two years. Islamic State became public enemy number one, and IS was no friend of the Taliban. In jail, a couple of inmates decided they were IS and then everybody, including the Taliban and the gangsters, wanted to kill them. Compared with the Taliban, I didn't like Al-Qaeda, who only wanted to tear the world down, and the IS prisoners, who were kept separate, were even bigger fuckwits. They wouldn't talk to me. Nobody, least of all the Taliban, liked them. Outside, in some parts of Afghanistan, there was a three-way fight between the government, the Taliban and IS, which was resolved when the government pulled out and left the Taliban to massacre the IS guys.

The news about Mullah Omar's death, which broke in 2015, caused a massive rift among the Taliban in prison. A lot of friendships got broken because some of them had known and not told the others, which put their noses out of joint. They should have just said he was dead when he died. For morale, the lying did them untold damage. A figurehead means everything to them; he grants permission. Without leaders, the Taliban were a fraction of the threat.

Bin Laden's death and the assumption of Mullah Omar's death from about 2011 led to the gradual release of Taliban prisoners anyway. By 2015, the majority of them were gone. In my last year in jail, I was alone with kidnappers, drug smugglers and gangsters; not a single Panjshiri, mind you, because the NDS were mixed up in the drug trade and protected their own.

Around the same time that Bevan was released, Hakemi appeared in the doorway to my cell and said, 'I'm leaving today.'

'Oh yeah?' I said. 'Where are you off to?'

'Back to the mountain.'

We said our goodbyes and that was the last time I saw him.

The government was releasing Taliban prisoners on condition that they guaranteed not to go back to fighting. The Taliban, including Hakemi, said, 'Of course we won't fight.' And off they went—to fight.

On the first Eid holiday after his release, I phoned Hakemi in Pakistan.

'Is this the painted man?' he said.

'Yes. Is this the man in the mountain?'

'Yes.'

'And which mountain would that be?'

'Not a mountain near you.'

I wished him Happy Eid.

He said, 'Are you still a communist or have you converted yet?'

'I'm still a communist.'

'That's a shame. How long are you going to be in there for?'

'I don't know.'

'Well, if you're still there when we get back to power, I will let you out and come with you to Australia. Will they let me into Australia?'

'Probably not,' I said. 'I'm pretty sure you'll have a hard time getting in.'

'That's a pity. I would have liked to see the kangaroos.'

'But we've got this little island resort called Nauru where they might let you go.'

He laughed. We had discussed Australia's immigration issues over the years. Hakemi couldn't understand why Afghan emigrants didn't just go to the Australian embassy in Kabul and apply properly. 'If doing it the proper way is easier and wouldn't cost you money, why not do it? Stupid people—Afghans always want to do it the hard way.'

I could have said the same about him.

16

A soldier in prison

I wasn't in Afghanistan to save the world but to discover it. I was there for nearly nine years, all but one of which I spent discovering the inside of a prison cell. In enduring that, I ended up discovering a bit about the world but even more about myself.

What made me the kind of person who could survive those years in an Afghan prison? It's probably the thing people ask most now that I'm out, and also the thing that I'm least equipped to answer. Short answer: I just did it by breaking each day into little bite-sized pieces. The long answer is much more difficult.

I think of myself living alone in that cell for so long, the last two-and-a-half-years of it without a friend or anyone to have a proper conversation with after Bevan and Hakemi. All the prisoners whose conversation had sustained me inside—Glen, the Nigerians, British Paul, Bevan, Andre,

261

Hakemi—were gone. That left a long stretch when it was just me and my daily routines. One push-up closer to freedom.

If I had grown up as a more social being, it would have been harder. But solitude suited me and enabled me to deal with tough physical conditions. The kid who was on his own in Pol-e-Charkhi was the same kid who had dragged himself out of bed on his own at dawn from the age of seven or eight to milk the cows. It was cold and you got kicked. And yet I got it done. When I had free time, I would take the dog and piss off into the scrub for hours on end. My parents were okay as long as I was back before dark. I would go out and explore the bush by foot, or ride a motorbike when I was a bit older. I learnt how to shoot and drive when I was very young, and it was no big deal. I'd been raised to be self-sufficient and didn't need a lot of conversation to keep me going.

If I didn't want to interact with any Afghans, I didn't have to. I pulled my head in and stayed separate. In time, they as good as forgot about me. The guards would get to the point where I would have to remind them, at midnight, to lock my door. They knew that even if it was left unlocked, I wouldn't come out before four in the afternoon when I went outside for my exercises. Locking it was for my safety, to keep others out, not to keep me in. I got them adjusted to my clock, rather than me adjusting to theirs.

In those two-and-a-half-years between Bevan's leaving and my own release, I was never happy. Fuck no. But I was stable and comfortable and in a routine. I never let my guard down. I always made sure my door was shut when I was in my cell. I had a phone, but kept it out of sight. If I used it, I sat with my back to the door so that nobody could see me if they looked into the room. An old phone I still had, I left for the cops to use. They weren't allowed to use phones in the prison. I said, 'Listen, I'm going to put this phone in the foyer. If you want to ring your family, put your SIM card in and it's there.' They appreciated that. Some of them would want to talk and come in for coffee.

As I withdrew from other humans, I made an unexpected new friend.

Back when I'd been working in Iraq, we had a cat at the house in the Green Zone. Rob B told us to get rid of her, so we took her with us on one of our trips to the airport and dumped her there.

Two weeks later, she turned up back at the house. The boss was now pretty impressed by her internal homing system over a distance of several kilometres, so he allowed her to become the house cat. Otherwise, we shot the feral cats around the compound that were feeding off the rubbish piled in the street. We joked that one big ginger tom had belonged to Saddam Hussein. Because of its colour and its enormous melon, which was the size of a brick, we called it Pumpkin Head. It hung around among the rubbish and we were told to shoot it, but good old Pumpkin Head just shrugged off the .22 bullets and moved on.

Growing up in the countryside, I had shot feral cats all my life. Dad had a passionate love for birds, which he painted and drew, and he said Katie and I could kill cats without needing to ask permission. When our family first moved from the bush into Port Augusta, my cattle dog killed every cat within a two-kilometre radius, which left us with some explaining to do.

But while I was in prison in Afghanistan, I developed a new relationship with the species. I don't like killing cats anymore. I feel I owe them.

While I was in Block 10, a cat adopted me. Commandant Hershod used to feed her, and when he left the prison, she knew where I lived and turned up in my room. She became my best mate.

I named her Shitty the Cat. She was pitch-black in colour and had a very strange personality. I fed her and talked to her, and she probably learnt English. I was waiting for her to talk back. She killed all the mice and cockroaches that came into the room. When she started having kittens, they would hang around for ages until they got big enough that she kicked them out. The male kittens used to lurk outside, mewling for sympathy, but she wouldn't let them in. The female kittens just went off to do their own thing. Shitty was with me for three years and had a litter in my room in each of those years.

She hated Afghans, probably because, apart from Hershod, they mistreated her. Animals who had contact with westerners usually chose them above the Afghans, who would try to kick them. She stood her ground staring at them, which forced them to back down. Her loathing for them became an early warning system for me in my cell. I would be on my bed reading, and suddenly she would growl. I'd go to the door, to find an Afghan guard or prisoner hovering.

'How did you know I was here?' the guard said.

'Cat told me.'

That freaked them out.

The cat did some weird shit. She would sleep all day, and then wake up and go off her head, chasing things that weren't there. She spent a lot of time watching me. After Bevan had left, I had pushed his bed up against the wall and converted the underside into shelves. The cat sat up on top of that bookshelf and watched me. On my last day in the prison, when I packed up, she howled in agony. *What's he doing?* She knew.

Shitty the Cat is probably still there. I wouldn't be surprised if she runs the place now.

————

Authority in Block 10 at Pol-e-Charkhi was maintained, for the longest period that I was in there, by Commandant Hershod. In the military, it's believed that you can judge the morale of a unit by how they carry themselves, and unusually from what I saw of Afghan authorities, Hershod believed that too. He would tear into the guards if they turned up with their boots unlaced. If they fucked up in any way, he had them out doing drill. I had never seen that in Afghanistan, either inside the jail or outside. The guards hated it, but it instilled discipline and that's why I liked him. During my time, he was moved in and out of the position for reasons I never figured out, but whenever he left, the wheels fell off, and guards on duty were in thongs or sandals or in *shalwar kameez*, smoking hash or opium, standards not being enforced. But then Hershod's return would lift things again. You could see it before your eyes, a living example of the importance of leadership.

Hershod was a man I could deal with. When Bevan was still there, Hershod said, 'If you've got phones, hand them in and I'll let you use them once a month.' We complied, and because we were well behaved, Hershod let us use them once every two weeks, then once every ten days, and then once a week. Bevan and I didn't cause him any problems, and he eventually let us use the phone whenever we wanted.

But as soon as Hershod was replaced, my phone disappeared. The new commandant said, 'Hershod stole your phone.' When Hershod came back for his next tour of duty in the prison, I told him what the other commandant said and he went off his nut. He was ready to kill that guy, and eventually Roz Mohammed, Hershod's deputy, told me that the other commandant had stolen it.

Hershod had principles, but he was no angel. My initial internet phone had been a Nokia C1, a rip-off of the Blackberry, but that was confiscated when I left Block 4. After I'd been in Block 10 for a while, Ivan brought me a good smartphone, a Samsung Galaxy. Hershod noticed that it was better than his phone, so he did a swap: he got my Galaxy and I got his. It was a condition of him letting me use it at all.

His last replacement, in 2016, let me keep Hershod's old phone. It was stored overnight in the commandant's office and when I asked for it they brought it to me. One day, one of the guards was fucking around with it and dropped it. The phone was broken. I blew up and they went about replacing it. An English-speaking cop that I got on well with, called Admir, took it into town and got it fixed. Later Kim brought in a cheap smartphone, which I still have. I got good internet, thanks to a Mister Simcard subscription which my sister topped up with $20 every few weeks. Kim and Ivan also used to chuck money onto it, or send me phone credit directly. There were also ways of using Virtual Private Networks (VPNs) to cut down on the data I was using, increasing security and bypassing the telecommunications blocks that applied in Afghanistan. I used secure messaging with people outside, on WhatsApp for a while, and then other applications.

While other prisoners might walk around the corridors or the exercise yard using their phones openly, I kept mine out of sight and used it only when I needed to. The threat of violence, so all-pervasive in my first year in the system, had eased when I had moved in with the Nigerians and then when I was with Bevan. We had had a certain safety in numbers. But now that I was alone again, I had to be constantly on my guard, and in the periods when Hershod wasn't in command and maintaining discipline, there was a sense of anything goes.

Anyone who knew me in the army would be shocked, I think, to hear that I appreciated and even admired this authoritarian leader. I never really objected to authority itself, it was the way people used it.

For more than a decade, I loved every part of being in the Australian Army, but I began questioning things in 2000, when we undertook two overseas peacekeeping trips to the Solomon Islands and East Timor.

In the Solomon Islands, on Operation Plumbob (which the diggers renamed Operation Bumjob), we spent all of our time on the HMAS *Kanimbla* bobbing about in rough seas, doing a lot of physical training and on the return trip shooting a lot of unused ammunition, which we couldn't take back into Australia due to government regulations, off the back of the boat. The young crew were brilliant, enjoying paying me out on their internal radio show after I had walked straight into a Black Hawk helicopter on the deck, breaking my nose. In my defence, it was painted in camouflage.

It was a potential problem, the lack of wars to fight in. We always wanted to be in it. It's an alpha culture. You want to be on top of your game, and you want a chance to prove it. When guys didn't have that outlet, they would fuck up. In the early 1990s, we would be training, training, training . . . and for what? To go to Tully to fight the Vietnam War all over again? You want to be on tools, you want to do something.

East Timor could have been a fulfilment of our years of training, but instead the UN the peacekeeping mission was run with ineptitude. I quickly came to dislike the compromised way it worked: the UN not doing anything, driving past villages they were supposed to be helping, sitting in air-conditioned LandCruisers. The attitude of the hierarchy pissed me off as well. The Australian Army was stacking people there so they could get gongs and move up into nicer offices. It turned into a big CV-building exercise for the officer class.

There was pretty much a constant stream of bullshit from HQ types, but a flashpoint for me was when the battalion was selected to test a new antimalarial drug. Before we left Townsville, the CO of the company said, 'Taking the drug is not compulsory, and some of you will get placebos. But if you don't volunteer to take it, you're not going.'

That's not really volunteering, and the CO later denied what he'd said in front of the whole battalion.

It was hard to work out the logic. If the drug was not dangerous, why were American medical corps people rolling up to watch our reactions after we had taken it? A Canadian airborne unit, after taking it in Somalia because the Americans would not, went loopy and began committing suicide and killing innocents. Immediately there were problems among us. We took it every Sunday, and on Monday they couldn't get any work out of any of us. It affected us in different ways. I felt deeply depressed, but others were homicidal, fighting with their mates. Everyone had bad dreams.

I went to our company medic and asked to be taken off it and put on an older, more predictable drug, doxycycline.

It was like they went out of their way to fuck us up. A good mate of mine was one of the control group and given a placebo. Great, he wouldn't get the after-effects of the new drug. But then he went to East Timor and contracted cerebral malaria. Twice a year, even now, nearly twenty years later, he gets attacks from the malaria and can't control his body temperature.

Around the time of those two trips, I started to lose faith in the institution I had served all my life. The esprit de corps among the NCOs was as strong as ever, and that was what kept me there when I was posted, kicking and screaming, to the School of Infantry at Singleton as an instructor.

To my surprise I enjoyed it, and found I was good at it. With September 11 bringing Australia into the 'War on Terror' and the invasion of Iraq on the horizon, there was a change in attitude to being an infantryman. In peacetime, kids often joined the army to become a loadie or a vehicle fitter or some kind of tradie, so that they could take that skill to the outside world. The army was just a means to an end. But fundamentally, the infantry is the core of any army. Everyone is there to support you. At the end of the day that's what it's about. With that attitude now back in place, we were given the resources to effectively train soldiers for the battalions.

I rediscovered my enthusiasm while I was training those kids, but my old bugbear—the attitude of the hierarchy—had not disappeared, only gone underground for a while. It was always ready to resurface.

After two years at Singleton I was posted to 3 Combat Support Regiment (3CSR). I was in the Recon platoon, which shared a more relaxed attitude than most. As luck would have it, our RSM (Regimental Sergeant Major) didn't share this attitude, coming from Signals Corp rather than infantry. At some point it was obvious there was going to be a clash of cultures.

We came back to our 3CSR HQ one Thursday afternoon from three weeks away, cleaned our gear, our weapons and our vehicles, and knocked off. In a tradition dating back to the 1960s, Friday was the day off, the 'make-and-mend' day. Because we'd just come in from an exercise, our hair was long, we were dirty and stinking and unshaven, and we changed into physical training (PT) gear before we repaired to the boozer on the Thursday night for some weekend beers.

It was seven o'clock in the evening, we were buggered, and the unit RSM cracked the shits, going off at us. He screamed at us 'grunt fuckbags', attempting to humiliate us in front of the young signallers—who, to be honest, looked a little embarrassed by him and would later come up and apologise to us.

His behaviour was typical, but what can you do? We left our beers and went back to our lines. We cleaned ourselves up, just as he ordered, before coming back and finishing our beers in front of him. He was still going off. If he'd only come over and had a quiet word with us like an RSM from an infantry battalion, we'd have gone and got cleaned up without a fuss and it wouldn't have been a problem. But what got him off was being able to treat us like shit in front of his signallers. For us to be reprimanded as NCOs in front of junior ranks, it damages the system. If the RSM thinks we're fuckwits, the privates under him feel entitled to think we're fuckwits too.

What sent me over the edge was hypocrisy. Later that night, that RSM was pulled over by the cops and breathalysed. He was charged with DUI. Not a word was said about it within the unit. He was a protected species. Meanwhile, we were still getting our arses kicked for having a beer without shaving. I thought, *You want to make me a sergeant so I can hang out with fuckbags like that? No, I'm out of here.*

So I left the army. This, combined with the deterioration of my relationship at the time, made me think about where I was going with my life. The answer wasn't much of a jump—I began working as a contractor.

———

I believed in authority when it was effective, and when I was living under the rule of Commandant Hershod, I appreciated his effectiveness. With him controlling the cops and acting reasonably towards me, for months at a time no violence would happen. A riot might break out, making it rough for everyone for a couple of days, but being shut inside didn't affect me other than being unable to run my laps.

When he had to undertake reprisals, Hershod was brutal. I had seen him deal with those gangsters who set the fires, and he performed clusters of executions at different times. He executed the teenaged kidnappers who had given us grief over our shorts and a bunch of Taliban all in the one go. The guards took them into the kitchen building, where there was a strong exposed steel pipe running across the ceiling. The guards threw a rope over that and dragged the kidnappers in, kicking and screaming. Then the guards would lift the prisoners up onto one of the trolleys they normally used to push food from cell to cell. When the prisoner was standing on the trolley and had the rope tied around his neck, they kicked the trolley out from under him.

An American-made Humvee ambulance was waiting outside to take the bodies away. During this spate of executions, there was a fat prisoner who the guards couldn't lift onto the trolley. So they got the ambulance, which had a winch on it, tied him to that and winched him off the deck. That was how they hung him. Fuck! Was that how I would have been dealt with if my death sentence had been carried out?

17

Seven years

From the day Kim Motley took on my case, she worked tirelessly on two fronts. One was to nibble away at the length of my sentence. When the *ibra* went through, my death penalty was commuted to life imprisonment. Later in 2011, the Afghan government handed out a widespread list of sentence reductions to prisoners. The reasons were often pretty bogus, more about showing the world what good Muslims and merciful people they were, but I got the benefit of these and my life term was cut to twenty-five and then twenty years, with a further two years off after the *ibra* was received.

Over the following three or four years, as Afghanistan made an effort to clear foreign prisoners out of its system, I saw people on lesser convictions than mine leave Pol-e-Charkhi after reductions or pardons from the government. President Karzai used to issue pardons left, right and centre, but they all required money, and if you didn't pay people, you didn't get reductions, even if they were presidential decrees.

Kim also pushed the government to reassess the prosecution case against me, which was obviously weak. The gist of what she told them was, 'This was all wrong and if you took it to a western court it would have been thrown out.' Her arguments went all the way up to Ashraf Ghani, who became president in 2014, and she told me that when this intelligent man saw my case, he would agree that it was best to sort it out before Afghanistan lost more face. That's what drives them, Kim said: not right and wrong but the image of right and wrong.

When Ghani took over, he gave fewer pardons and reductions, but those he gave actually went through without the need for massive bribes. By 2015, when I had been in jail for six years, the reductions I had been given meant that I only had a couple of years left to go. Kim kept going to meetings with legal officials saying, 'Rob's only got this much time left. Let him out.' It was still an embarrassment to Afghanistan that they had one last westerner in Pol-e-Charkhi on a murder conviction that should have been overturned on the ground of self-defence, but Kim had to give them a way of releasing me that would not look like an admission of failure.

The second front Kim was working on was a change in the law relating to foreigners in Afghanistan. With the help of Majell, one the Australian consular staff, and Matt, the Australian Ambassador in Kabul, she got the ball rolling on a new law under which, if the country of origin asked for a prisoner to be handed over, the Afghan government was obliged to do it. This wasn't a means of securing release, but of allowing the prisoner to serve time in more humane conditions in their own country. There was an international precedent for this. The Australian David Hicks was arrested on terrorism charges in Afghanistan in 2001 and then banged up in Guantanamo Bay for years before the Americans handed him over to Australia, where he completed his sentence in Adelaide. Steve Kenny, the South Australian lawyer who had represented Hicks, had made contact with my family quite early in my term, and he helped at the Australian end throughout. Steve took a back seat to Kim, but he was always helpful as an intermediary with the Australian government and the Australian embassy in Kabul. After I got out, I went to Adelaide and had a few beers with him. 'I haven't done all that much,' he said. I replied: 'You've done a whole lot more than other people.'

Kim played a forceful role in getting that law changed, which has a great flow-on beyond my case. If the same thing happens to another westerner in Afghanistan, their own country will be able to get them out. This wouldn't free them in itself, however, and I didn't want to be released just to be sent to a prison in Australia. I told Kim that I would leave Afghanistan a free man or not at all. And this was where Kim's work on that first front of undermining the original prosecution case came to my aid. The Australian embassy recognised that mine was a case where not only should I be freed from Pol-e-Charkhi, but I should not be in any prison at all. And in the end I got a full pardon, even if the Afghan government wanted to save face by not making a public announcement about it.

I was not really aware of these negotiations blow-by-blow. In my last couple of years in prison, I got through with a hell of a lot of push-ups! Sticking to my routines, enduring one day at a time, making myself as safe as possible in my little bubble: those were my priorities right up to the last day.

Kim was very careful when she came to talk to me. We met in a conference room. She didn't like being alone with the police, and she also didn't want them in our meetings. 'I want to talk to Rob on his own,' she would snap at them. They would hang around looking dopey. Most of the NDS guys were failed spooks anyway, trying to practise their English by talking to her. She was good at ignoring them.

She told them, 'You can't be in the room.'

They said, 'Yes we can, we're NDS.'

She said, 'Okay,' and she and I just sat there, saying nothing, until eventually they grew bored and left. Then Kim and I would rattle through what we needed to communicate.

Occasionally, I would clash with Kim. Sometimes I was too impatient and threw a tantrum, and at other times we would argue over some small point and then not talk to each other for weeks. We argued about anything. I'd say, 'You said you'd have news by this point!' She would fire back: 'I never said that!' After a particularly fiery argument, I found out that a guy had tried to carjack Kim's husband and had shot him point-blank in the face, back at their home in North Carolina. Fortunately he survived the shooting, but Kim hadn't told me. Ashamed, I rang and apologised to her. Those were some of the ups and downs in our relationship, which was not quite the typical lawyer–client thing. (By the way, the carjacker ended up trying it once too often: when he bailed up a small African American woman, she pulled out her Glock and shot him in the face. Karma.)

Kim was amazing. Sometimes she had nothing for me but came anyway. After her husband got shot, I didn't see her for nine or ten months. But if ever I texted her a message saying, 'I've got the phone,' she would call me straight back.

———

In mid-2016, I was fairly settled in my routines with my close confidant, Shitty the Cat. She'd had a litter of kittens which I was helping her to look after. One day, a prison guard who wanted to show me how tough he was killed one of the kittens. Admir, the young English-speaking guard I was quite friendly with, had that guard dismissed, but there was no mileage for him in taking the side of the lone western prisoner.

Admir was a good guy. I'd been helping him with his English over the previous months. After the incident with the kitten, he came up close to my bars and whispered, 'There's a group of guards who want to get you.' I was being blamed for the dismissal of the guard who had killed the kitten. The ridiculousness of it made me angry, but it was one more potential threat I had to deal with.

Three months later, after an argument, Admir got stabbed by a prisoner. I heard a scuffle going on down the corridor, so I padlocked my door. The next time I went outside I saw a lot of blood on the floor. I was told that Admir had been stabbed in the guts by a prisoner as soon as Admir opened his cell door. I was told that he was dead, which sent me into a new low. I had lost the one guard who would stand up for me.

A few nights later, I was speaking on the phone to Kim, telling her that I was really angry and hoping she would have some good news for me. She was very cagey and wouldn't give anything away, but just as I was ranting on again about how pissed off I was, she interrupted me.

'What's the first meal you want when you come out?'

'Er, I dunno.' I couldn't come up with anything. 'Why do you ask?'

'No reason.'

The next day—31 July 2016—was just another day. I'd got up and done my exercises and had just given myself a shower when a guard came to the door of my cell and said, 'You're going.'

'Fuck off,' I said. 'I'm busy, I can't be bothered with you right now.'

'You really are,' the guard said. 'Come up to the office.'

I was still sceptical, having seen Bevan go through this charade time after time, returning disappointed and depressed to his cell a few hours later. I had to follow the guard to the office but was not up to packing all my things. When I went out into the corridor, who should show up but Admir, in civilian clothes. I was stunned.

'I thought you got killed!'

'No,' he smiled, 'but I got very sick.'

'What are you doing here?'

'They told me that you would not believe them when they said you are leaving. They brought me in because you will believe me.'

It was true. Since Commandant Hershod's last departure, Admir was the only person on the prison staff I trusted. I thanked him for everything, and told him that if I didn't come back, everything I had left in my cell was now his.

Coming to terms with the idea that I might actually be getting out—but most of me still tensed-up for disappointment—I followed the guards to the prison office. Ivan was there, looking as deadpan as ever. But no sign of Kim.

'What's going on?' Ivan said.

'I dunno. What are you fucking doing here?'

'You tell me.'

Apparently Ivan had found out, through Kim via the trucking company he was now doing security for, that I was actually leaving. It was seeming more and more real, and yet still impossible to believe. We sat there, making small talk, until Kim arrived with the paperwork.

She was escorted by a fixer from the embassy called Aziz, and Jess Donati, a reporter with *The Wall Street Journal*. Since being burnt so badly by Jeremy Kelly, I was coloured for life against journalists, and Kim had shielded me from a Danish documentary team who had come to the prison to film Bevan for a documentary called *Motley's Law*. Kim was a superb media manager, and when she introduced me to Jess earlier in 2016, she said, 'When you come out, you'll need to get your side of the story across.' I didn't see the point, but Kim persuaded me.

The fact that Jess knew Kim had got her part of the way into my confidence, but when she'd first made herself known to me, she also said she was doing a story on my old boss, John Allen. 'If you don't want to talk to me that's fine,' she said the first time she phoned me. 'I just figured you might like someone to talk to for a change.' That night, I checked with Kim, who said, 'She's deadly serious, she's good.'

Jess had said, 'Next time I come, I'll bring some coffee.' And then she turned up, sure enough, with a big jar.

I said, 'Thanks, but what do you want?'

'I don't want anything, I just thought you'd like it.'

So we sat and talked shit. Nothing to do with John or the company. We clicked, and she turned out to be genuine. She risked her neck to deliver a jar of coffee because she said she would. That went a long way with me.

The one interview I gave was to Jess, and I didn't regret working with such a smart and principled operator. We made an agreement that she wouldn't write a word of my release interview until I left Afghanistan, and she stuck to it.

If she ever gets into shit over there, I would go back and get her, but I have the sense that she can look after herself.

Jess came in very helpful on the day of my release. As usual, there had to be photos with the commandant of the prison and people from various government ministries wanting to show how instrumental they'd been in such a humane act as releasing me. It was typically Afghan, and typically chaotic. When an official said, 'Is anyone here from the Australian embassy?' everyone looked around. Jess, of all people, got up and signed my release on behalf of the embassy. I was laughing and Kim was telling me to shut up. Ivan was shaking his head in bemusement. Bullshit baffles brains, every single time.

I tried to call Katie, but couldn't reach her. Unknown to me, she was five hours' drive north of Alice Springs, with no hope of phone contact. It was only after she got back into range that she discovered a WhatsApp message I sent her, saying simply: 'I'm out.'

Katie then called Mum and Dad, who were on a holiday with friends in Darwin. She had to wait for a few minutes of Mum describing events on their trip before she was able to butt in and say, 'Rob's out.' They had no idea, it happened that quickly.

My head was spinning to find myself being driven on the streets of Kabul for the first time since I'd been moved from Tolkeef to Pol-e-Charkhi years earlier. On our first night, I went with Kim to an Italian restaurant near the British embassy. I had a topside steak and a Fosters, and after the years of plain food and no alcohol, it tasted . . . pretty disgusting, as only Fosters can!

There was no rush in getting me out of the country. My visa paperwork would take some days to sort out, and we all agreed that it was best for my mental health to take it in slow, careful stages. Ivan took me to the compound of the security company he was working for, where there were a few spare rooms and I could stay for a week. In retrospect, it was a sensible approach. The other people living in the house were security contractors, and, among my own sort, I could gradually let my hair down. It was a good thing for me to get my head straight. If I'd tried to get out of Afghanistan on the first day, I probably would have punched someone at the airport. But the fear of suddenly being grabbed and thrown back into prison was always there. I made plans for escaping from the house, in case the police stormed in. The first night I was there, I was in the kitchen. Kim came in and said, 'What are you doing?' I was looking for a knife to borrow, in case I had to fight my way out.

During those days, I even did some bodyguarding work for Kim, driving with her when she had to attend a meeting at a company where her task was to give the staff the bad news that they had been made redundant. She drove around Kabul by herself, and I was able to witness her doing her job. She was one tough lady.

Beyond that inner circle, no westerners in Kabul knew I was free. A few days after my release, I had to go with the Australian ambassador and a consulate staffer to meet with the Afghan deputy minister for foreign affairs. The Aussie ambassador thought I was one of the security guys! The bigwigs were talking about me, and the minister was saying, 'Mr Langdon's on his way today and will be introduced to you.'

Kim butted in, saying, 'No, Mr Langdon is this guy sitting right here.'

The minister and ambassador, to their credit, recovered pretty quickly.

It was quite funny, being incognito. I was taken to a barbecue, where I found myself talking to an Australian reporter who was not at all popular.

'And who are you?' she said very self-importantly, as if she needed to know my position in order to rate whether I was worth talking to.

'I'm just passing through,' I said.

'Ah, you're one of those wannabe James Bond idiots. Boring.' And she turned away.

So she missed that story. I hope when she realised it, she was fucking fuming.

A week after I walked out of my cell in Pol-e-Charkhi, I was back at Kabul International Airport, the scene of my arrest. It was now called Hamid Karzai International Airport.

Five minutes in 2009, and I might have got away on that minibus and onto the plane to Dubai. Now I was going to Dubai again, but this time on an Emirates flight with Kim by my side, her laptop hooked up to wi-fi, getting hammered by requests from the media to talk to me. I was out. But was I free?

18

Surviving

'You seem so normal!'

I hear this a lot. People can't believe that I can go through what I went through, and hold down a conversation or go to the shops and buy groceries.

'That's because no one's trying to kill me,' I say.

But I'm joking. I'm not normal.

After my release, I was pretty fried. I went to stay with my family in Port Augusta and found it hard to cope. When I was seventeen, I hated it and got into trouble. Nowadays, it's still a small town and people know our family, and when I went back there in late 2016 I felt that I was in a fairly unpleasant fishbowl.

Like a lot of regional Australia, Port Augusta has a growing problem with crystal methamphetamine use. I would go out for walks and find myself passing groups of users standing on street corners or in the yards of their houses. I just wanted them, or myself, to disappear. One day I was going by one of these packs when someone called out to me, 'How ya going?' It wasn't friendliness, it was boredom, baiting me to see what would happen.

'Better than you, mate.'

It was what I said in jail whenever an Afghan asked me how I was. *Yeah, better than you.*

I was twenty-five metres down the road before they realised what I'd said.

'Hey, come back here, we'll fuck you up!'

I thought, *Whatever.* And kept walking. They're like dogs: brave when others are around or when they're behind a fence. I decided then that I'd had enough of Port Augusta. It was a matter of time before I bit back.

The last straw in Port Augusta was after a day when I went out for a run. To add weight and make the workout more strenuous, I ran in army boots with an old chest rig. I had run on that road, towards the army camp and back, since the 1980s. After my run, as I was walking into my sister's house, a cop car pulled up.

'We got a report from someone who saw a suspicious guy in military gear running on the road,' they said. Someone had reported me as a suspected terrorist.

Fuck that gave me the shits. People don't understand the threat. A bigger danger to them is some random off-his-head clown coming up from behind and punching them out. Or a pub bouncer beating up patrons. When it comes to terrorism, the attacker is not going to be a bloke wearing a chest rig bowling up to an army outpost. It's going to be a lunatic in a car. When I was in prison, as I whiled away the hours exploring the dark web of the internet, I came across an IS recruiting conversation. One recruiter was telling another,

'Our people don't have access or the skills to use firearms, so get them to kill people with cars. Nobody can ban cars.' And that's how it has turned out.

I was ranting about these sorts of things to my sister when it struck me: I can't live in this town anymore.

I'm not even sure I can live in Australia anymore. It might be part of my post-prison psychological state, but I don't feel at home in a community that is so insulated from the world I have known. Seven years in an Afghan prison can do that to you. Getting on the train for the first time in Adelaide freaked me out. I don't like people standing too close to me if I don't know them.

I am aware that this is not a million miles from any soldier's struggle to adjust after coming out of an operational tempo. People don't understand what you've done, and they have no experience to compare it with. For soldiers, the only time the public shows any appreciation is around Anzac Day, which is really just a day for them to get on the piss. Soldiers are committing suicide because they're so used to being around their mates and protecting them, and can't handle moving back into a world where they get told off for not wearing a seatbelt by some overdressed, over-equipped policeman who hasn't ever done anything. Why are the cops in Australia dressed like they're about to invade Poland? What's the point of wearing a lot of gear that will intimidate people? When I was involved in low-level operations with UN peacekeeping forces and the like, one of the first things we were taught was, in one-on-one confrontations, put your gun down. Half of the clashes between police and civilians, I reckon, have started since the cops began wearing all that kit. When they present as aggressive, people react differently to them.

In February 2017, I went to South Africa to reconnect with my old friends, and began to feel that that was where my future lay. South Africa is great for people like me: the beer's cheap, it's a great lifestyle, and you don't need to feel you're a freak for walking around with a knife in your pocket, because everyone has one. In Cape Town, through Manuela, I met some coloured gangsters who she was teaching to tattoo so they could earn a proper living. One of them, an older guy in his fifties, talked about things in South African prisons he'd experienced, and I talked about things I'd seen in Afghanistan. It was strange but interesting. We were saying essentially the same things—what happens when a lot of men are locked up in a box. For reasons I can't quite explain to myself, I have always felt at home in South Africa: the unique mix of first world and third world mentalities appeals to me. It was easier for me to fit in, where there's a level of edginess, than in Australia where everything felt so quiet and controlled. Back when I first went there in 2004, while I was doing the Close Protection course, on the first night, before the course had even properly started, a British instructor came running into the restaurant where we were having dinner and said, 'There's been a stabbing in one of the townships. We need two guys to come with us to give us a hand.' Most of the guys in the course thought it was a stitch-up. They weren't taking it seriously. A Zimbabwean guy, John C, and I put our hands up and went. It was real, all right. There had been a fight and a stabbing, and a guy had been knifed in the neck. John C and I helped with the attempted resuscitation on him. Sadly, we couldn't save him, but we did our best even after we knew he was going to die. When I'm in Australia, I never get the sense that I am going to be urgently needed for a situation like that, whereas in South Africa it can happen at literally any moment.

It was also in South Africa in 2017 that I started to feel that I was on the mend. A friend of mine there said, 'You're the same as before, but you're more present.' She was right. Before prison, I was always thinking about what I had to do next. It was how I'd been trained. Downtime between operations was about getting ready to go out again. *I've got to do this prep, get new boots, get ready.* Now I'm not so agitated about the next thing. Belinda said I'm the same person, but a lot more willing to connect with people than I was before. This might be my problem in Australia: I am seeking human connection, but the sort I need is hard to find.

So maybe I am getting better, but more of the people I want to connect with are in South Africa. By the time you read this, I might be living over there. Right now it feels far more like home to me than Australia.

Less than a year since my release, I'm aware that I am still very much in a readjustment phase. I struggle for focus and direction. When you're out of jail, it's surprising how you miss the simplicity of your routines. Moving towards an unspecified future is not so clear-cut as it was inside when I always had my eye on the next task I had to get done. And relating to family and friends, I have had to pull myself up a few times since getting out. Being in a prison among fuckwits you don't like, including police, you're still nice to them because it makes life easier. You can get people to do what you want if you act like their friend. So, when I was in prison, I never gave everybody my full self. I gave them a mask and was guarded against giving them anything they could use against me. I was friendly and open until I didn't have to be.

It took me a while after my release to work out if I was still doing that. Am I genuine, or am I back in the habit of masking and using people and bullshitting, a habit that built up over all those years? I think I'm getting it under control, but one of the reasons I had to move away from my family was because, with the best possible intentions, they forced me to question my own authenticity too soon. That has been one of the most difficult parts of the readjustment.

I have not sought professional help, other than reading a lot.

I've become so self-reliant, I only want to deal with my problems on my own. If you're not going to bullshit, start by not bullshitting yourself. But the downside of this is that you can turn yourself into an island for the rest of your life.

One thing I can say squarely is that I do not struggle with my conscience over killing Karim Abdullah. Three times I asked him to move on, and his response was to threaten my terp and then me with his pistol. I thought he was going to shoot me, and I reacted. That's how my dad brought me up, and it's how I was trained in the army. It's what the law allows. You give people fair warning, and if they want to fuck with you, you step up and you don't hold back. I had to be that way in jail and it saved my life again and again.

If I had my time over, I'd do the same with Karim, and I would conduct myself in jail the same way that I did. It's hard for someone who hasn't been there to understand the complete lack of empathy in those situations in Afghanistan. It is what it is.

I feel the same way about Commander Haussedin, who did whatever it took to get where he was, and who I believe was instrumental in getting me arrested and locked away. I have no respect for him. Unlike the Taliban, he wasn't fighting for something he believed in. He was just a gangster.

My story is my honest testimony. I never got the chance to provide my account in a court of law, and to lose more than seven years of your life after never getting to speak, well, that leaves you in a pissed-off state. I'm not saying this is exactly how everything happened, but I am providing a sincere account of how I saw it. I do want people to know what a cesspit of corruption that their countries fomented in Afghanistan, and I want them to see how it affected one Australian who was there. I know I'm not a good person and I don't need validation. I've done good things and bad things. Take it or leave it, it doesn't bother me.

A few days after I got out of prison, Ivan, my great stead-fast mate, sat down with me and said, 'You've done all this and you've survived. No matter what the reason you ended up in there, it's incredible. What we do to get into Special Forces in three days, you've done it for seven years.' I took that as the biggest compliment anyone could pay me.

What I am proud of is that I survived. I got through more than seven years of being in the worst prison in the world, without becoming a drug addict, without compromising myself, without turning into a person I am ashamed of. I am intact.

Epilogue

Here's how close I am to the rest of my life.

Minutes. Maybe ten, maybe fifteen, stand between me and the people getting off the plane. I arrived Bangkok International Airport an hour earlier, the trip in an Uber from the city taking almost an hour itself through Bangkok's notorious peak-hour evening traffic.

It's been almost a year since I got on another plane and left Afghanistan for good. My old boss, John Allen, is still there, essentially a prisoner in a compound somewhere in Kabul. His alliances with warlords of dubious reputation has finally caught up with him, with several of the Afghans who worked at Four Horsemen being implicated in atrocities against Taliban prisoners whilst in a militia group he set up for the US and Afghan governments. Too paranoid to return to the US, and more than likely to be arrested if he left the compound, only Four Horsemen's Kenyan finance officer remains with him as he struggles to clear his name. His Afghan 'friends' charge him ridiculous prices for rent, food and, of course, the facilitation fees to get even the smallest things done. This is Afghanistan, after all, and that is how things are done. Or not.

The anger is still there, simmering away below the surface. I've learnt to manage it, turning it into something positive. A month ago, I came to Thailand and started training at a Muay Thai camp—nothing like getting your arse kicked all day, every day to re-adjust your attitude. All that's done with now and for the first time in my life I'm going to have a proper holiday. No prepping for the next job, or coming back off leave early because I'm bored—just beaches, good food and rest.

I'm not going to know what to do with myself. Going to need to work on that . . .

The masses of Chinese travellers are filing out through passport control now, coming to buy cheap knock-off luxury goods and experience a culture not dissimilar to their own. The irony is that most of those goods I've seen here are made in China. That brings a smile to my face. They could have saved themselves a trip, but Thailand is probably better than the provinces. Some of the larger tour groups all have matching jackets, and are led by a guide with a matching flag. They look like dragon dancers in a Chinese New Year parade.

Among the Chinese are the western backpackers. I'm trying to work out nationalities from accents and the hiking gear brands. Most are in their twenties to thirties. Those on their first trip stand out the most, belongings clutched to their chests as they are thrust out into Third World chaos. The old hands, packs covered in flag patches of the places they've been, push through the throngs of people to change money or get a new SIM card before heading to Khao San Road.

Eventually the crowd begins to thin out, save a few stragglers or those patient enough to wait out the initial crush. I had already figured out I would be waiting around to this point, but the OCD kicks in so I go to check the arrivals board for the third time. Sure enough, the plane I'm waiting on has landed.

As I wander through the last few people meeting friends and family, a familiar face framed by chestnut hair strides through the door, wearing an old red flannel shirt, ripped jeans and vintage '80s Reebok sneakers, her backpack hanging off her shoulder by one strap. There are tears in her green eyes, but that smile is as brilliant as ever as I walk towards her.

'G'day, B,' I say.